VICTOR KUGLER
The Man Who Hid Anne Frank

VICTOR KUGLER

The Man Who Hid Anne Frank

As told to and edited by Eda Shapiro

Compiled and edited by Rick Kardonne

gefen

publishing house בית הוצאה לאור

JERUSALEM • NEW YORK

Layout: Marzel A.S. — Jerusalem
Cover Design: S. Kim Glassman
Photos on the cover: Toronto Telegram, 1979

ISBN: 978-965-229-410-4
Edition   1 3 5 7 9 8 6 4 2

Gefen Publishing House Ltd.
6 Hatzvi St.
Jerusalem 94386, Israel
972-2-538-0247
orders@gefenpublishing.com

Gefen Books
600 Broadway
Lynbrook, NY 11563, USA
1-516-593-1234
orders@gefenpublishing.com

www.israelbooks.com

Printed in Israel   Send for our free catalogue

With gratitude to Nathan Jacobson of Toronto and Tel Aviv,
whose generosity made this book possible

Contents

Preface

For over twenty years beginning in 1972, I had written numerous articles for Canada's two major Jewish publications — first, *the Canadian Jewish News*, and then, *the Jewish Tribune* (formerly *the B'nai Brith Covenant*) — on both cultural and political topics. Through my writings I was fortunate to have met many leading representatives of Jewish communities in Canada, Israel and elsewhere, as well as non-Jewish political leaders such as the last Soviet president, Mikhail Gorbachev, who significantly shaped — for the better — the fate of large Jewish communities.

One of these representatives was Harry Wolle, who represented Israel's Herut-Likud party in both his hometown of Toronto and Israel, where he lived in the 1970s and early 1980s. In the spring of 1996 he introduced me to Irving Naftolin, a distinguished Canadian Armed Forces veteran who took part in the liberation of France, Belgium and the Netherlands from Nazi German tyranny.

One June day in 1996, I bicycled to Irving Naftolin's apartment in the heart of Jewish Toronto, North Bathurst Street, where he showed to me a truly unique "find" which I immediately recognized as being of historical importance. It was the typewritten memoirs of the man who hid and supported Anne Frank, her family, and several family friends: Victor Kugler, the Mr. Kraler of her diary, who lived his last twenty-five years (1955–1980) in Toronto. Irving's late wife, Eda Shapiro, interviewed Victor Kugler from 1969 to 1973, and wrote these memoirs as he dictated them to her. After her passing in 1992, Irving Naftolin took it upon himself to have her work published.

Our mutual friend Harry Wolle brought Irving and me together, so that not only would these memoirs be compiled into a book, but the details of this shy man's life would be discovered and exposed for the world to see. Without the perseverance and courage of Irving Naftolin and Eda Shapiro, important

1

questions about Anne would never have been answered. Thanks to Irving Naftolin, the story of the missing link, Victor Kugler, can, through means of this book, be brought to light so that the complete story of Anne Frank can finally be revealed.

— Rick Kardonne
January 2008

Introduction

On a pleasant cloudy evening in May 1978, inside the sanctuary of Toronto's Beth Tikvah Congregation, a tasteful, modern brick synagogue on suburban Bayview Avenue in the north of Toronto, a significant cultural and historical event took place. It had wide-ranging implications for the world Jewish population and for people of goodwill everywhere.

From the Diary of Anne Frank, by Canada's leading, internationally recognized composer, the Czech-born Oskar Morawetz, was performed by a Canadian Broadcasting Corporation orchestra. Oskar Morawetz was himself a Jewish refugee, having been fortunate enough to escape just as the Germans invaded Prague. For this work, he had taken Anne Frank's immortal words and set them to his hauntingly dissonant music. *From the Diary of Anne Frank*, one of the most important symphonic compositions of the twentieth century, made him world famous.

The music was appropriate for the Anne Frank family, because it had no distinct melody yet was compelling. It would not have been appropriate to have used Jewish folk melodies from Eastern Europe, because the Frank family, while proudly Jewish, came from an assimilated, German-Jewish cultural milieu which eschewed Jewish folk roots for the radical, avant-garde dissonances of enlightened German modernists such as Alban Berg and Paul Hindemith. It was not meant to be shocking. The shocks to the Frank and the van Pels families (whom Anne called the van Daans) were to come after the time of the diary, when the Gestapo discovered the Secret Annex and deported them to the death camps of Auschwitz and Bergen-Belsen. Rather, the music had a subtly dramatic feeling of approaching terror tempered by stubborn hope.

A Canadian operatic soprano named Belva Spiel, who was at the time well known on Toronto's serious Jewish music scene, sang the solo role of Anne

Frank. Being a mature woman, Belva, of course, could not, and was not meant to, convey the impetuous youth of thirteen-year-old Anne. But in the historical context, with her seasoned reflectiveness, Belva Spiel perfectly captured the spirit of ironic tragedy that Anne feared the most, but, against all odds, hoped would never actually happen.

Many leading cultural and political dignitaries representing all walks of life in Canada's most populous province were in the audience. But the focus was on a significant guest, without whom the diary of Anne Frank would never have been written. He was the man who had sheltered Anne Frank from the ever-watchful, prying eyes of the German Nazi Gestapo for two years, thus permitting her to record her remarkable chronicle of human courage against extreme adversity.

Much has been said about the heroic roles played by Miep Gies and Elli Vossens, the two office girls, and Jo Kleiman, who tried their hardest to conceal the Frank and van Pels families and Dr. Fritz Pfeffer in the Secret Annex. Their roles must be acknowledged and honored. But the undeniable truth remains that at the time, Miep Gies and Elli Vossens were only in their early twenties. Through no fault of their own, they lacked the administrative skills necessary to run the Frank spice import business — a business that had such precious human treasures to sustain, in the most dangerous environment possible. An experienced, seasoned, mature individual was needed to run this business at a profit and at the same time to supervise the smuggling not only of business supplies but also of food, water and other provisions for the Secret Annex's hidden Jewish inhabitants — all under secretive, siege conditions.

To most of the world outside of Toronto, this man was known by a pseudonym: he was the "Mr. Kraler" of *The Diary of Anne Frank*. He was the "missing link" in the Anne Frank saga. If it had not been for him, the Frank business would have collapsed financially within a month. The Franks and van Pelses and Dr. Pfeffer would have starved soon afterwards.

Nearly thirty-four years after the Secret Annex had finally been betrayed and the Gestapo had dragged its inhabitants off to Nazi death camps — from which only one, his former business partner, Otto Frank, by sheer chance, was to survive — the gentleman became the guest of honor at an event six thousand geographical miles — and, figuratively, light years — from the hell of Holocaust Europe.

The guest was a quiet, distinguished, modest Austrian-born naval veteran who had moved to Amsterdam after World War I. After World War II, like Oskar Morawetz and many other Europeans of all walks of life and political persuasions, he had moved to Toronto. He had chosen Toronto as his home because of a sister-in-law who lived there. Like many other Europeans, he also ultimately chose Toronto because, while it is a big city, it has many quiet suburban family neighborhoods, which, although they are close to down-town, lack the frenzied congestion of the largest American cities. This gentle-man, who was not himself Jewish, had originally come from Austria, the nation that gave birth to many of the war's most notorious Nazis — not only Hitler himself, but also such monsters as Eichmann, Globocnik, and Seyss-Inquart, the fanatically cruel German governor of the occupied Netherlands. Together with Raoul Wallenberg, Oskar Schindler and Sempo Sugihara, he had become one of the world's most famous Righteous Gentiles — those unique individuals who, at great risk to themselves, had saved Jews during the Holocaust.

This gentleman had taken one of the greatest risks of all. He was neither a diplomat nor a prominent industrialist with connections. He was not an academic; in fact, among all the walks of life from which Righteous Gentiles came, academics are noticeably lacking. Nazi Aryan racial superiority theo-ries, which in large part had made the Holocaust respectable, had been in vogue among European academics for at least fifty years prior to Hitler's accession to power.

Rather, this man was an ordinary business manager with a simple, humane conscience, all too rare in that worst period of human history. As Otto Frank's business partner, he saw the Frank family forced into hiding when Germany occupied Amsterdam and he thought it only just, right and natural for him to manage the Frank business and conceal the Frank and van Pels families, and the dentist Friedrich Pfeffer, in the "Secret Annex." After the Jews were discovered and deported to the death camps, he himself was arrested and sent to a series of German forced labor camps, from which he eventually escaped.

Following the war, like so many other Righteous Gentiles, this gentleman remained supremely modest about his bravery. Only when he came to Toronto in 1955 was it revealed that he was indeed the man known as "Victor Kraler" in the diary. Like all the other names outside of the Frank family, it was a pseudonym, used for security reasons. When he was taken to see the hit play *The Diary of Anne Frank* in 1958, at what was then Toronto's only large commercial theater, the Royal Alexandra, he was so embarrassed at being portrayed on stage that he swore that he would never again watch a dramatization of his life.

That year, German journalist Ernst Schnabel wrote a biography of Anne Frank (*Anne Frank: A Portrait in Courage*), which included the wartime memories of several survivors, including this gentleman. In it, his experiences were described in rather general terms. The biography did not receive wide distribution, and the gentleman himself chose to remain low-key, speaking about his wartime experiences only in small, friendly environments like the Toronto Jewish day school system.

It was at one of these lectures, in a Jewish school in 1969, that Mark Shapiro, a Toronto university student who was planning to immigrate to Israel, heard this gentleman speak. He told his mother, Eda Greenberg Shapiro, whose family had itself only narrowly escaped the same environment in which the Franks and van Pelses and six million other Jews were murdered by the will of Adolf Hitler. It so happened that Eda Shapiro was working on a book consisting of interviews with the many Holocaust survivors who had moved to Toronto.

And so, for four years, she interviewed this gentleman extensively about his life and experiences before, during and after the Holocaust. It was thanks solely to her that the detailed totality of his life became public knowledge. Gradually after these interviews, he began to "open up" on a local level. He was written about in the popular daily *the Toronto Telegram* and later in a two-page article by Eda Shapiro in the *Toronto Sun*. He was the subject of an hour-long prime-time TV documentary by one of the Canadian Broadcasting Corporation's best recognized producer-directors, Harry Rasky, entitled *The Man Who Hid Anne Frank*. Twenty years after his unease at seeing the Broadway play on Anne Frank at the Royal Alexandra Theatre, the gentleman, now in his late seventies, consented to attend Oskar Morawetz's symphonic adaptation of the diary. It was a performance that left him greatly moved and that he openly praised.

At Eda Shapiro's behest, this gentleman was presented with one of Israel's greatest honors: citation as a Righteous Gentile at Yad Vashem on the hillsides of Jerusalem, the world's leading memorial to the victims of the Holocaust.

Just prior to his death in 1981, he was honored in Canada by North America's longest governing mayor, North York, Ontario Mayor Mel Lastman, together with Ken Taylor, the Canadian ambassador to Iran who saved American hostages from a more modern would-be Hitler, Ayatollah Ruhollah Khomeini (whose name is the same as that of a biblical persecutor of Jews, Haman).

Now, after the untimely death of Eda Shapiro, her work has been completed, and is finally being presented to the world.

The real name of this hero whom Anne Frank called "Victor Kraler" is Victor Kugler.

This is his story.

But it is also the story of Eda Shapiro, who devoted the latter years of her life to revealing his heroism.

As much as possible, the book consists of memoirs of both Victor Kugler and Eda Shapiro. They include not only Victor Kugler's early life and his experiences in shielding the people in the Secret Annex, but also his experiences under German incarceration after the Gestapo captured and deported the Franks and van Pelses. The reminiscences of two other Torontonians who knew Mr. Kugler well are included. They are Evelyn Wolfe, a prominent layperson in Toronto Jewish organizations, and composer Oskar Morawetz, who met Mr. Kugler through Otto Frank while researching the material he used to compose his symphonic work in Anne Frank's memory. Supplementary chapters have been written by the compiling editor to round out the historical background of Dutch Jewry and the Dutch nation during the Holocaust period from a Jewish perspective. A few relevant details about the lives of Otto and Anne Frank, and Victor Kugler in Toronto after the war, have also been added.

It is not the purpose of this book to reproduce the actual diary of Anne Frank — that has been done many times before. Jon Blair's superb recent film, *Anne Frank Remembered*, from the book by Miep Gies, is one of the truest and most powerful portrayals to date of Anne Frank's personification of the epitome of the Jewish tragedy of the Holocaust.

The present book seeks to appropriately commemorate the legacy of Victor Kugler, who in his turn epitomizes the Righteous Gentile. The

Righteous Gentiles were too few in number to stop Hitler, but their legacy from the Holocaust is aptly memorialized at the Yad Vashem memorial in Jerusalem, and represents humanity at its most noble during a time when much of mankind, through commission or omission, sank to its lowest ebb in history.

It is to Victor Kugler and the Righteous Gentiles that this book is thus dedicated.

Chapter One

Eda Shapiro Meets Victor Kugler

Eda (Greenberg) Shapiro was born in Ukraine in 1918, at the height of the Russian Civil War, which followed the Bolshevik Revolution. Her family moved to Rumania and then immigrated to Toronto, Canada, in 1927.

The Russian Civil War was one of the bloodiest periods in Jewish history, surpassed only by the Holocaust, the Roman destruction of the Second Temple, and the Chmielnicki massacres of 1648. The anti-Bolshevik White armies led by Generals Petlura and Denikin massacred tens of thousands of Jews, mostly in the Ukraine, between 1918 and 1922. Petlura was assassinated in Paris in 1926 by a Jewish student named Sholem Schwartzbard. When the French court was told of the full extent of Petlura's monstrous crimes, Schwarzbard was acquitted.

Eda was a good student, who first learned office work, then turned to journalism and writing.

In 1945 she married Sam Shapiro. In 1949 she had a son, Mark. These memoirs, written in 1970, give pertinent details about her own background. They are preserved intact:

> But for the grace of God, I, too, could have been a victim of the Holocaust. I could have been one of the six million Jews who perished as a result of that colossal tragedy. I am no stranger to persecution and terror.
>
> After the Russian Revolution of 1917, there were a number of years of great unrest in the Ukraine, where I was born. Anti-Semitism flourished, and pogroms, sparked by Generals Petlura and Denikin, kept recurring. I was a very small child at the time. I can just

remember being completely wrapped in a blanket and my father carrying me in his arms. In my mother's arms, similarly wrapped, was my baby brother.

I heard shots in the air. A bullet pierced my blanket and missed me by an inch. I said: "Papa, why are they shooting at me?" This traumatic experience is one of my very first memories. My late parents told me that we would all have been killed, but for the kindness of one of my father's friends, a Gentile. We fled to his home for shelter. He hid the four of us in a large closet. His teenage daughter, looking on, said to him: "Why don't you get rid of these Jews? If they are found here, we'll all be killed." Her father answered: "If you fear for your own life, go and stay with your married sister. This is my friend and his family and I mean to give them shelter."

He sheltered us until we were ready to escape to Rumania.

I don't know that man's name, or, indeed, if he is still alive. But surely he must be considered one of the "righteous" — that rare and wonderful breed of Gentiles who save Jews at the risk of their own lives. As I said, we escaped from the Ukraine to Rumania. We had been there only a few years when my parents again saw the writing on the wall. There was growing anti-Semitism in Rumania, led by Professor Alexander Cuza. There were bloody anti-Semitic riots in the streets. Homes were burned and synagogues were desecrated. Jewish students and professors were bodily thrown out of classrooms.

My parents decided to uproot our small family once more, to seek a haven in Canada. We first glimpsed its friendly shores in February 1927.

I have heard that the small Rumanian town we left was completely destroyed during World War II.

Toronto became a major destination for Holocaust survivors. There were several reasons for this. For a short time right after the war, Canada, probably to atone for its heartless earlier anti-Jewish immigration policy (well documented in the book *None Is Too Many* by Toronto York University Professors Irving Abella and Harold Troper), admitted more Jews than did the United States. Another reason was that the areas of initial Jewish settlement in

Toronto were less congested and physically more attractive than their eastern American counterparts. This became particularly true in the early 1950s, with the development of northern Bathurst Street. Today, this remains one of North America's most vibrant, all-encompassing, proudly Jewish main thoroughfares. Here, Jewish refugees found a familiar lifestyle, but in a cleaner, more modern, much safer, more suburban environment than the one they had left behind in Eastern Europe. Eda Shapiro continues:

> Many members of our family were lost in the Holocaust: uncles, aunts and cousins. One of my cousins was forcibly separated from his wife and three children. After the war, the Red Cross helped him find his family. He was reunited with his children, but his wife had perished in the Holocaust.
>
> In an uncle's large family a male cousin was the sole survivor. In an aunt's family, a female cousin was the only one to escape with her life.
>
> These two cousins decided to get married and are now living in Israel. They might have made something of their shattered lives, except that my female cousin, in addition to losing her whole immediate family in the Holocaust, also lost her sight. For her, most places are now the same: as dark as her past.
>
> Any wonder, then, that I have such empathy with survivors of the Holocaust.
>
> I have read many books about this monstrous atrocity and I find it hard to believe that such beastliness could have existed. Then I notice a blue number on the arm of a survivor and I know everything I have read is true.
>
> I am convinced that there could never be enough written on this gruesome subject. I shudder when I think that within a few decades, less than seventy years at most, there won't be a living eyewitness on earth to record the greatest atrocity in the history of mankind: the Holocaust.
>
> I am determined to seek out as many survivors as I can and help them write down their terrible experiences for the record, and indeed for posterity.

These words were written nearly a quarter-century prior to the Steven

Spielberg video documentation of Holocaust survivors. How much more urgent the task is now, as the first decade of the twenty-first century draws to a close. Eda Shapiro continues with a personal statement:

> I don't believe that the passage of time makes a crime less heinous. Indeed, the greatest atrocity towards mankind in general and the Jewish people in particular becomes even more shocking when viewed through the cold eye of history.
>
> I firmly believe that most people are basically good. I believe that they prefer justice to persecution and murder. Furthermore, I am sure that the more we awaken man's conscience by writing about the Holocaust, the more chance there is that mankind won't permit a recurrence of this most heinous of crimes.
>
> I had an excellent Hebrew education and I am proud of my Jewish heritage. I gravitated towards Zionist clubs, and as much as I loved Canada, I longed for Zion. As a teenager I even seriously considered moving to Israel (then Palestine) and settling on a kibbutz. The idea of a communal life, where each gave according to his capabilities and each received according to his needs, strongly appealed to me, and the thought of Jews living in dignity in their own land was uppermost in my mind.
>
> However, my mother (of blessed memory) was seriously ill with heart disease. If I had left home at that time, I might have jeopardized her very life, for we had a wonderful relationship. As a result, my dream of living in the ancient homeland of my ancestors had to remain in abeyance.
>
> Then came the Nazi Holocaust, and a third of my people were ruthlessly murdered in Hitler's gas chambers and crematoria. Possibly as a partial atonement for that great tragedy, the world permitted the establishment of the State of Israel in 1948.
>
> I thought: "Perhaps, at last, our wandering will cease. Perhaps the death of six million of our people will be partially avenged."
>
> But just prior to the Six-Day War of June 1967, I, along with most of my Jewish brethren, noted with alarm that Jewish life had become cheap once again.
>
> Once again, history began to repeat itself. On May 26, 1967, King

Faisal of Saudi Arabia declared, "Our aim is to exterminate Israel!" Nasser strangled Israel via the Gulf of Aqaba, and was prepared to throw every Jew in the state into the sea.

Meanwhile, as the "debating society" on New York's East River expressed "alarm" and many nations "voiced their concerns," every Jew in Israel and the Galut (meaning Jews living outside of Israel) had visions of another Holocaust for the Jewish people — this time a complete one.

That did it for me and my family. We knew that but for God and the State of Israel, the Jewish people were alone. This was the catalyst for the Shapiro family. We decided that the best answer to the "Jewish problem" was a strong aliyah (immigration to Israel). We determined that as soon as possible, the three of us would settle there.

Our son Mark was advised that he could best help Israel by bringing with him the best Western education he could get. Since he was majoring in English, with a view to a teaching career in a university, for him that meant a PhD in English. It would take at least until 1974. Then we would all move to Israel.

I was working on a book entitled *Tales of the Holocaust*, as told to me by the survivors.

It was thanks to the preparation of this book that Eda Shapiro, who had herself been saved by a Righteous Gentile, met Victor Kugler:

> One evening in 1969, my son Mark, who was majoring in English at the University of Toronto, came home from a lecture and said excitedly: "Mom, I've just met Victor Kugler. He is the 'Mr. Kraler' of *The Diary of Anne Frank*. I just heard him speak at Associated Hebrew Schools. Wouldn't he be a fascinating subject for one of your *Tales of the Holocaust*?"
>
> I was immediately caught up in Mark's excitement and within minutes I was speaking on the telephone with the teacher who had arranged the lecture.
>
> I asked her how I could get in touch with Mr. Kugler, and she said: "I'll give you his telephone number. My husband and I just drove him home. You can probably reach him right now."
>
> I did, and Mr Kugler graciously agreed to give me material for a

story. After several interviews it became evident that his experiences were numerous enough to fill a book of their own, and I feel honored and privileged that Victor Kugler gave me exclusive rights to handle his memoirs. It took numerous interviews, phone calls, tapes, mailings, copyright negotiations, etc., from the time we first met in Toronto in 1969, until 1971, when I moved to Israel. After that, we continued by correspondence until 1973.

Since I am writing his story in the first person, I am restricted from going into detail about my own impressions of the man. I feel I owe it to my readers to give them a more extensive portrait of him. What does he look like? How does he impress me? What are some of these endearing qualities? Hence this third-person profile of Mr. Kugler.

Profile of Victor Kugler

Victor Kugler is of medium height, slender and academic in appearance. He has sleek, dark hair, with just a touch of grey at the temples, and he has beautiful manners.

When you first meet him he seems inscrutable, though his clear blue eyes can be quite penetrating. However, when you get to know him better, you learn that he has a keen sense of humor and a warm personality. You also become aware that these same clear blue eyes often show a mischievous gleam and that his slow, warm smile becomes more and more frequent.

He is soft-spoken and calm. I can readily see how a man of Mr. Kugler's quiet strength and determination could help to hide eight people (Anne Frank, her family and friends) for two years, right under the nose of the German occupying force. I can understand how, as a prisoner, he was able to practically take over the running of a German forced labor camp, help his fellow prisoners, and, in his own words, "cheat and outwit the Nazis." I am not surprised that he was able to forward vital information to the Dutch Underground — information that was very useful to the Allies. And when he made a break for freedom, even though the risks were tremendous, it was just what one would expect of him.

Now, at age seventy, Mr. Kugler's unlined face and vigorous appearance belie his age.

When I got to know him better, I found that under that calm facade was a very warm and sensitive human being. I became aware that delving into his past and reliving his experiences was quite painful for him. Once, when he was telling me about a particularly moving incident, I noticed that his voice was more emotional than usual; he reddened and turned his head away from me. I realized that he did not want me to see the expression on his face. I strongly suspected that he was trying to hide a tear or two. I said, "Excuse me, Mr. Kugler. I'd like to check my notes for a few minutes." It was a ruse, of course, to give him time to compose himself. When I looked up from my notebook again, he was his usual calm self. I hope he will forgive me for revealing this intimate glimpse of him. In those few moments he endeared himself to me, for I saw a warm and deeply sensitive human being.

Mr. Kugler is an avid reader and particularly enjoys history. He is fond of music and likes going to concerts. He also enjoys visiting art galleries. In the matter of art, he favors the old masters, especially his countryman Rembrandt. His favorite hobby is photography, which he takes very seriously. He has a well-equipped darkroom in his home. And he likes to travel.

I have the impression that one of Mr. Kugler's pet peeves is wasting time. I suspect he gets annoyed with people who squander time; and I think he has disciplined himself never to do so.

The following incident from his memoirs will prove my point about his views on wasting this most precious of gifts.

Mr. Kugler sent me many neatly typewritten notes, which helped me in the writing of his memoirs. The incident to which I refer happened at a very crucial time in his life.

Mr. Kugler had escaped, together with several other prisoners, from a forced labor camp. They were hiding in a brick kiln and had to wait until it was dark before they could venture further. I was amused to read in his notes, and I quote: "We had a lot of time on our hands, so I opened up my bundle, and started to darn all my socks and mend my clothes."

To me, this was a bit of comic relief in a very tense situation. I had a vision of several unfortunate human beings on a desperate bid for freedom. How impatiently they must have waited for night to fall and how terrified they must have been lest they be caught! Their very lives were at stake. In the midst of all this, Mr. Kugler was sitting calmly darning his socks. The former business executive (he had been general manager of the firm "Kolen and Company," which was owned by Anne Frank's father, Otto Frank) was absorbed in the task of mending his old, torn clothes. The incident revealed so much to me about Mr. Kugler, the man. In the face of grave danger, he did not cringe: instead, he did something positive. And he is so unassuming and modest that he told me about it. He saw nothing odd about a man of his former station darning socks.

Mr. Kugler dresses very well. He is always immaculate and his clothes are well coordinated. I can quite understand that while he was making a break for freedom, and hoping soon to reach his home town of Hilversum, he wanted to look as neat as possible. So he tended to his socks and clothes.

And of course, he proved what I had suspected: namely, that he hates wasting time. He believes in making good use of it.

Through numerous personal interviews with him and the copious notes he sent me, I have come to the conclusion that Mr. Victor Kugler is a very courageous and remarkable man indeed.

Chapter Two

Holland — A Historical Background

As Eda Shapiro implies, the Dutch are known as a nation of Righteous Gentiles. Yet the sad truth remains that the Jews of Holland suffered a far greater loss of life than those of any other German-occupied country in Western Europe. How could this have been?

Approximately 75 percent of Dutch Jewry was murdered by the Nazis. Of a previous population of 140,000, only about thirty-five thousand survived. By contrast, almost all *eight thousand* Danish Jews survived the German occupation of Denmark, although it lasted as long as that of Holland. Perhaps the larger size of the Dutch-Jewish population worked to its disadvantage? But, even in Rumania, the home of the overtly anti-Semitic Iron Guard which conducted murderous pogroms in Jassy, half of the Jewish population of 600,000 survived, a higher percentage than in the Netherlands. Being part of a small Jewish population was in itself no guarantee of safety: half of Norway's eighteen hundred Jews failed to survive and more than 90 percent of Estonia's five thousand Jews were murdered. Meanwhile, in neighboring Finland, the entire Jewish population of two thousand survived. In Bulgaria and Fascist Italy (where there were substantial visible and identifiable Jewish populations in the capital cities of Sofia and Rome, as there was in Amsterdam) the survival rate was nearly 80 percent. (These figures are from what is now considered the leading scholarly work on the Holocaust, Lucy Dawidowicz's *The War against the Jews.*)

In order to fully appreciate the bravery of Victor Kugler, the question of the fate of the Dutch Jews must be addressed by focusing not only on the Jewish community itself, but also on the Netherlands' prewar historical background. Even more particularly, we must take into consideration the unenviable direct rule under which Holland found itself during the German occupation. Overall, it was perhaps the harshest outside of Eastern Europe.

The Prewar Dutch Jewish Community

Following the Spanish Inquisition, the Netherlands became the first European place of refuge for those ousted Spanish Jews who did not go to Morocco. In the early sixteenth century, Holland was the most prosperous country in continental Europe because of its strategic naval trading position, and the Spanish Jewish refugee merchants were welcomed for their international connections.

The ruling Calvinist House of Orange looked kindly on the Jews, regarding the wealthy Sephardic merchants as a key economic asset. Oliver Cromwell, who was also a Calvinist, maintained friendly links to the Orange monarchy despite his strongly republican political philosophy. Hence he permitted Jews to resettle in England when he was in power. When William of Orange became the English king after winning the Battle of the Boyne in Ulster, he enlisted the support of Sephardic Jewish families who had found a safe refuge in the Netherlands. This initial royal alliance cemented a tolerance towards Jewish life that persisted in the Netherlands until the 1930s.

The Sephardic foundation of Jewish life in the Netherlands was broadened by consecutive waves of Ashkenazic immigration from Germany and Eastern Europe during the seventeenth, eighteenth, nineteenth and early twentieth centuries. The Dutch Jewish population eventually grew to 140,000. By the beginning of the twentieth century, there were eighty thousand Jews in Amsterdam, mostly Ashkenazic. Two-thirds of them were recent Eastern European immigrants. They settled first in the near east side of the city in a neighborhood that resembled New York's Lower East Side, London's East End or Montreal's Boulevard St. Laurent, as they then were, rather than the besieged ghettoes of Berlin, Warsaw and countless other Central and Eastern European cities.

East Amsterdam, with its multi-floor, narrow, steep-roofed red brick houses, was poor, congested and teeming. But there were never any pogroms, special taxes, identification badges or police repression, and there was an economic way out of the ghetto via business or the professions.

Many of the Ashkenazic Jews worked in the diamond industry, a tradition that persists today in the Flemish capital of Antwerp. They made a relatively quick move out of East Amsterdam into South Amsterdam, a more comfortable area filled with picturesque red brick houses lining numerous quiet canals. Although it contained a large Jewish population, it was not exclusively Jewish. South Amsterdam became the closest refuge from Nazi Germany in the mid-1930s. Among its German-Jewish refugees was a Frankfurt businessman in the prime of his life named Otto Frank.

Jewish refugees from Germany in the 1930s were greeted by what seemed to be an atmosphere of tolerance. Both Sephardic and Ashkenazic groups maintained thriving synagogues and organizations, and an active, free Jewish press. There were a fair number of Dutch Jews in Holland's upper echelons of commerce, culture and the professions.

Underneath the surface, however, this tolerance was fragile.

Holland, Denmark, Finland and the UK —
The Fundamental Difference

Ironically, the fact that the Netherlands essentially lacked an independent military tradition ultimately worked in the Jewish population's disastrous disfavor.

Denmark, though it too was small in size and population, had, in its past, consisted of a mighty empire. During the ninth century, it had occupied part of England; during the eighteenth, it had fended off the British Royal Navy. More recently, the Danes could not forgive Germany for arbitrarily annexing its two southern states, Schleswig and Holstein, during the early Bismarck years. Finland, just a year before it was conquered by Nazi Germany, had successfully fended off Stalin's invading tanks. National resistance to foreign conquest, from the very top, was a Danish and Finnish tradition.

Nazi Germany conquered Denmark in April 1940, one month before it conquered the Netherlands. King Christian X remained in the Amalienborg royal palace in the heart of Copenhagen and personally directed a national campaign, first of passive and then of active resistance. Those who have read Leon Uris's classic *Exodus* will remember that when the Germans ordered all Jews to wear the yellow star, King Christian, swearing that the Jews were all Danes and that one Dane was the same as any other, is depicted as having worn the first yellow star. Although the story is apocryphal, it does touch on the genuine spirit of active resistance that prevailed in Denmark. When the Germans finally ordered the roundup of the Jews, Denmark evacuated them to Sweden under the aegis of the king. The Danes even kept the Jews' homes in perfect condition until the end of the war.

Although Finland joined Germany in attacking the Soviet Union in June 1941, the Finnish government defied Germany's plans to murder its Jews. According to Lucy Dawidowicz in the above-mentioned work: "There were two thousand Jews in Finland. In a visit to Helsinki in July 1942, Himmler attempted to induce the Finns to deport the Jews, but Foreign Minister Rolf Witting refused to give the matter any consideration."

Britain was not conquered by Germany, but the British royal family provided an example of hands-on leadership and the principle of sovereignty in the face of Nazi aggression. The Luftwaffe concentrated its raids on the East End of London as opposed to Westminster or Chelsea. This may well have been because the majority of London's Jews were living there at the time. King George VI and Queen Elizabeth the Queen Mother personally walked through the streets of the East End as the bombs fell. This act of personal heroism not only provided solace to the Jews of England but also boosted the morale of the entire British population in withstanding endless blood, sweat and tears and ultimately, in defeating Hitler.

In contrast, the sovereign of the Netherlands, to whom the Dutch looked for moral guidance, provided no such example of personal, independent and if need be, military resistance to the Nazi juggernaut.

The historical tradition of the Netherlands (apart from the House of Orange's exploits in England) was that of mercantile accommodation, not that of an independent fighting spirit. It must be remembered that the deposed Kaiser Wilhelm II Hohenzollern of imperial World War I Germany had chosen Holland as his home, living there until he died in 1941, when Holland was under Nazi German occupation. In other words, the renowned expedient tolerance of the Netherlands could be a double-edged sword.

And so, on May 13, 1940, three days after the Germans invaded the Netherlands, Queen Wilhelmina, instead of remaining, as King Christian X of Denmark had done, fled to England. True, she declared London to be the seat of the Dutch government in exile. She vowed to fight against the invader. True, also, Prince Bernhard stayed behind to join Dutch armed forces still fighting in the province of Zeeland. But after a swift military defeat, he too left his homeland for England. Princess Juliana went on to Ottawa, where she gave birth to Princess Beatrix.

In the final analysis, the failure of the queen of the Netherlands, the ultimate symbolic sovereign, to remain in her country while it was under siege was a significant statement. It represented a lack of hands-on leadership at the very top, resulting in a state of confused impotence in a nation which she had, in truth, deserted in its greatest time of need. In other countries such as Poland and France, where the governments went into exile in England and in effect threw their homelands to the Nazi wolves, the lots of the Jewish populations were equally disastrous. In all of these countries, the German overlords and their local lackeys gained a free hand.

This moral vacuum allowed Hitler to subjugate the Netherlands more comprehensively than Denmark or Finland, where the rulers remained on home ground and served as symbols of national resistance. For Dutch civilians, accommodating and acquiescing to German rule thus became a more "natural" option; Hitler knew he could "get away with more" in Holland. Thus, despite some popular resistance in the Netherlands, the country was fundamentally in a far more vulnerable condition than either Denmark or Finland. It was much less able to protect not only its Jewish minority but also its Christian population against slave labor and other forms of repression.

The Rise of Nazism in Prewar Holland and the Dutch Reaction

Anti-Semitism appeared in Holland for the first time during the early 1930s. In 1931, before Hitler came to power, an engineer named Anton Mussert formed the Dutch National Socialist Party (NSB).

It was a carbon copy of its German equivalent. While the military contingent that provided the backbone of the German Nazis was lacking in the Netherlands, many of the NSB's adherents came from similar socio-economic groups to other elements of the early German Nazi Party. Amongst them were a surprisingly high number of schoolteachers and university academics who espoused an anti-urban back-to-the-land philosophy and advocated "Aryan" racial superiority doctrines. Mussert himself came from this academic background.

By the mid-1930s, the NSB had gained some support as a political party because it promised to remedy rising unemployment. But so did the Communist Party, which, Stalin notwithstanding, firmly denounced anti-Semitism. The Dutch Nazis received 8 percent of the popular vote in 1935, at the height of the Depression. But in 1939, when Nazi Germany had become more of a military threat, it received only 4 percent, a drop of half.

The Dutch government regarded the NSB, which in the 1930s had about thirty thousand members, as a danger to national security. In March 1933, it passed legislation forbidding military personnel to join the NSB. Later it passed a similar ruling regarding civil servants.

In 1936, both the Catholic and Dutch Reformed churches, much to their credit, prohibited their memberships from joining the Nazi party.

Nevertheless, even before the German invasion, the various levels of Dutch government were giving out mixed signals. As the tide of Jewish refugees into the Netherlands increased, there was mounting resentment amongst Dutch workers because unemployment remained high. The federal Hague authorities decided to intern refugees who had no money (most of them, as Jews were not allowed to take money out of Germany) in a camp in a northeastern Dutch province. This camp, called Westerbork, was later to be used by the Germans as a transit camp for Jews being deported to Auschwitz. Anne Frank and her family were initially sent there after their capture in August 1944.

On the other hand, the City of Maastricht, for example, took a more sympathetic position. Maastricht set up a central committee of representatives from various churches, to assist newly arrived Jewish immigrants and help them cope with issues of resettlement. The mayor of Maastricht served as chairman. One of the most courageous Righteous Gentiles of Holland, Arie van Mansum, whose remarkable story is documented in his biography, *A Friend among Enemies*, by Janet Keith, was chosen, at the age of nineteen, to represent his Dutch Reformed congregation on this inter-church council. He went on to save many Jews under Nazi occupation.

It is fair to say that Arie van Mansum's and Victor Kugler's sentiments represented those of a considerable number of Dutch people, especially within the ranks of labor and the clergy, and, to a degree, within a general cross section of the population. But it sadly must be said that these elements did not represent the influence-wielding "power elite" of Dutch society, some of whom had followed the royal family into exile, leaving a power vacuum against German might. Thus, in practical terms, once the physically and emotionally battered Dutch nation was put to the supreme test of contending with the harsh rule of German occupation, the Dutch Jewish population, while it elicited a degree of sympathy, found much of this sympathy to be powerless.

By 1940, roughly 5 percent of the Dutch population had overt Nazi sympathies. This might seem like a lot, and was comparable to prewar levels in Denmark or Finland.

But once the Germans invaded, given the rudderless condition of the Netherlands, the local Nazi element provided a surprisingly evil local root which assisted Hitler's macabre policies in assuming the upper hand.

The German Conquest of Holland

Hitler conquered Holland swiftly and violently. Once the royal family had left, he felt none of the constraints he had felt in Denmark. Thus, unlike in Denmark and Finland, the German conquest of the Netherlands was bloody.

Rotterdam was bombed to the ground on May 14, 1940, with multitudes of civilian casualties. The same fate was threatened for Amsterdam. Only a promise of complete subservience to German rule saved Holland's largest city.

The occupation of Belgium, Denmark, northern France and Finland was mainly military. Under it, civilian life was to go on as before, while Germany was to preside in all military and foreign affairs. The Netherlands, by contrast, was forced to endure a German civilian administration that was much more totalitarian and much more directly involved in the life of the average citizen. Holland's civilian administration was similar to the notorious German-run Generalgouvernement of Poland.

The Polish analogy was underscored by the appointment of SS General Artur Seyss-Inquart as Reichskommissar (imperial governor) of the Netherlands at the end of May 1940, two weeks after the conquest. This Viennese lawyer, whose role in the annexation of Austria had brought him to Hitler's attention, had previously served as second-in-command to the infamous Hans Frank, commissioner of the Generalgouvernement of occupied Poland. Seyss-Inquart was an avowed anti-Semite who was incomparably more intelligently sinister and thoroughly cruel than were the equivalent German military governors of Denmark and Finland, whose primary concern was defense against the Allies.

As security chief, Seyss-Inquart appointed another Austrian, Hans Albin Rauter, who imposed an iron rule enforced by German Gestapo and SS and Dutch Nazi police collaborators. Rauter was feared throughout the Netherlands.

Dutch resistance to this iron rule was well-meaning but initially futile, and suffered a major setback when a general strike was called by the labor unions in 1941. The reaction of Seyss-Inquart and Rauter was so intense and cruel that the forces of Dutch resistance were given a knockout blow from which they were not to recover for at least two years.

In the meantime, while there were Dutchmen who did all they could to save Jews under this reign of terror, there were others who openly collaborated, and many more who cooperated quietly.

Cornelius Suijk, who was the international director of the Anne Frank Foundation in Amsterdam in the late 1980s and, as of 1996, the international director of the Anne Frank Center USA in New York, said in Toronto in November 1989 (reported by Ben Rose in *the Canadian Jewish News* during the ninth annual seminar on Teaching the Holocaust) that 200,000 Dutch people collaborated with Hitler and that members of his own family failed to hide Jews when they were asked. Millions of his countrymen looked the other way when Jews were taken, he said:

> My father was a teacher and he signed a statement in two seconds
> that he was an Aryan, not realizing that a Jewish teacher in the school
> would be deported because he could not sign such a document. My
> father was inconsolable until he learned that the man had survived.

The fates of the Franks and the bravery of Victor Kugler and other Righteous Dutch Gentiles must be seen within this context of German Nazi rule at its harshest outside Eastern Europe.

Victor Kugler, born 1900

Victor Kugler and his mother Emma,
Austria, 1909

Victor Kugler, Austria, 1909

from the personal collection of Victor Kugler

Gelukkig Nieuwjaar

*New Year's card sent by
Anne Frank to Victor
Kugler (from the
personal collection
of Victor Kugler)*

Gewenst
door
Anne Frank

AMSTERDAM C.S.

Aan Den Heeren mevrouw
V. Kugler

Hilversum (N. H.)

Emmesserweg 56

Victor, Lucy, Charles (center), Eve, Aviva (granddaughter), Toronto, June 1978
(from the personal collection of Victor Kugler)

Victor Kugler's house,
22 Braeburn,
Etobicoke, 1970s
(from the personal
collection of Victor
Kugler)

Receiving the Righteous among the Nations award from Yad Vashem in Israel, 1972;
Victor Kugler holds his medal and Lucy the certificate (courtesy of Rita Visser)

Victor Kugler and Eda Shapiro, Toronto, 1970 (from the personal collection of Eda Shapiro)

Oskar Morawetz and Victor Kugler, Toronto, 1978 (courtesy of Oscar Morawetz)

Victor Kugler, 1979 (Toronto Telegram)

1973

Victor Kugler received this "Medal of the Righteous" in Toronto, Canada, on April 1973, by Consulate General Shmuel Ovnat. Recommended by Otto Frank and Eda Shapiro.

This MEDAL OF HONOUR was passed by the Knesseth, — the 'YAD VASHEM LAW' in August, 1953 (5713), to "Righteous Christians".

I have had the privilege of holding this Medal and examining it; and should like to describe it. It was struck specially for 'Yad Vashem' by the Israel Government, Coins and Medals. The medallion, made of silver, is encased in an olive wood box lined with dark blue velvet. On the right side of the box top, in silver, is the emblem of Israel: the seven-branched candelabrum. A tiny silver clasp opens and closes it.

Nathan Karp, the designer, inscribed the Talmudic saying: "He who saves a single life, saves the whole world". This is on both sides; — in French and Hebrew. One shows two skeleton hands, in concentration camp garb, reaching out beyond for world freedom. The other shows Yad Vashem, the hills above it, and a carob tree. A 'thank you' from the Jewish people, and the Recipient's Name.

Victor Kugler received this "Medal of the Righteous" in Toronto, April 1973

WESTSIDE CEMETERIES LTD

1567 ROYAL YORK ROAD
TORONTO, ONTARIO   M9P 3C4
TELEPHONE-416-241-0861
FACSIMILE-416-243-8824

ESTABLISHED 1892

1995

Dear Mr. Naftolin

From all the information you have given me,
I can see that the late Victor Kugler was an important man, and
a light for humanity at a dark time in our history.

I have no more information that would add to
your knowledge of this man, except that in answer to your question,
should Mr. Kugler have had a stone. There is a memorial bronze
marker on the lot for the late Victor & Lucy Kugler. I enclose a
photograph of this marker for your records.

Yours truly

John Barrett

But there remains no tombstone.

*Letter from the director of the cemetery where Victor and Lucy Kugler are buried,
including a photograph of the simple marker that designates Victor Kugler's resting place*

Chapter Three

Life before the Secret Annex

Eda Shapiro wrote about Victor Kugler's life in a fairly abbreviated form. The following is all she has to tell us on the subject:

The Early Life of Victor Kugler

> Victor Kugler was born on June 6, 1900, in Hohenelbe (known today as Vrchlabi, a ski resort town at the top of the Elbe River in what is now the northwest sector of the Czech Republic; in 1900, this was a part of the Austro-Hungarian Empire, in a German-speaking region that was known as the Sudetenland until the end of the Second World War). Victor Kugler started school there. The family moved to the Rhineland in Germany where he studied for four years. Then they returned to Austria.

Further details of Victor Kugler's early life are obscure, for he did not tell Eda Shapiro or anybody currently alive anything about it. Torontonians of Dutch-Christian descent who knew him, when asked whether he had told them anything about his life before he immigrated to the Netherlands, all said that he had told them nothing. Why?

If there was a key to this question, it was to be found eight thousand miles west of Europe, in a small Minnesota town called Waconia. Waconia is mostly populated by people of German descent. Josephine R. Mihelich, who wrote *Andrew Peterson and the Scandia Story*, a book about Scandinavian immigration to Minnesota that gained nationwide acclaim in 1987, is a spokesperson for the Waconia Heritage Association, a group of volunteers

who research and write the early history of the town. The Heritage Association initially had reason to believe that a pioneer settler named George
Kugler, who had settled in Waconia, was directly related to Victor Kugler. In
December 1994, as part of the association's research, Mrs. Mihelich wrote to
the Jewish Federation of Greater Toronto inquiring about a 1978 banquet that
had been sponsored by the Canadian Council of Christians and Jews to
honor Victor Kugler. This banquet will be described in greater detail later in
this book.

The descendants of George Kugler living in Waconia were unable to
provide any specific information on Victor Kugler. However, after a good deal
of correspondence between Mrs. Mihelich and various spokespeople in the
Toronto Jewish community, Irving Naftolin, Eda Shapiro's second husband,
received a letter from Mrs. Mihelich in which she wrote:

> When George Kugler's offspring saw Victor Kugler on TV, they were
> convinced there was a family resemblance. With that thought in
> mind, I knew I had to find out one way or another if a relationship
> existed. I have been researching and writing the early history of
> Waconia and George Kugler was an important part of this effort as he
> started the first lumberyard in Waconia in 1880.

Mrs. Mihelich went on to say that she had written to the Anne Frank House
in Amsterdam inquiring about Victor Kugler, but had received only the most
basic information concerning the dates and locations of his birth and death,
and the fact that he had moved to Canada in 1955. She goes on to explain:

> Although that information was disappointing because I had hoped
> his place of birth was in or around Auerbach or Nitzelbuch (southern
> German towns from where the Minnesota Kuglers were descended),
> I thought it possible George Kugler's missing uncle could have settled
> in Vrchlabi and started another branch of the family.

Mrs. Mihelich, through further lengthy correspondence, discovered and
contacted Iris S. Laskey of St. Mary's, Pennsylvania, a direct descendant of
John Kugler, George's father, who had been a village mayor in southern
Germany. Iris wrote Josephine Mihelich a detailed letter explaining that when
John immigrated to the US in 1846 he had left behind a brother whose name
and further life is unknown. In the light of George's physical resemblance to

Victor, it is possible, but cannot be proven, that this unknown brother was an ancestor of Victor's.

> Knowing I would regret it for the rest of my life if I did not pursue this matter further, I paid the Zamrsk Regional Archive in the Czech Republic to have a baptismal record search done as to the paternal genealogy of Victor Kugler and learned, after everything was translated that "Victor Kugler was born on June 6, 1900, in Vrchlabi. The father is not named on the certificate. The mother is Emilia Kugler [*Kuglerova, in the Great Slavic feminine style — ed.*], born November 16, 1877, in Jabolnc in Podjestedi." Emilia's parents were Anton Kugler from Plzen [*located in then-German Sudetenland*] and Wilhelmina Erben from Vrchlabi.

Was Anton a grandson of the unknown brother of Johannes (John) Kugler *Sr.*? (George's brother, who immigrated with George to the US, was also named John.)

Possibly so.

Following further research into the circumstances of Victor Kugler's birth, Mrs. Mihelich wrote to Irving Naftolin on February 28, 1997, confirming that

> Victor Kugler's birth certificate only lists his mother's name — Emilia Kugler — (aged twenty-three at the time of his birth) because Victor was born out of wedlock.

Mrs. Mihelich concluded her initial letter to Mr. Naftolin:

> Victor's birth situation will not cause us to admire or respect him less. May he rest in peace.

Mrs. Mihelich managed to contact a relative of the Minnesota Kuglers, named Helen Kugler, who was living in Toronto. Helen, on a trip to Germany, visited the area where George Kugler was born, but could find nothing linking George and the Waconia Kuglers with Victor. However, according to Stephen Speisman of the Canadian Jewish Congress Archives in Toronto, Victor Kugler had or might still have a brother (or half-brother) living in Germany. This brother's name, like that of John Kugler Sr.'s brother, is unknown.

There is always the theoretical possibility that the father of Victor Kugler may or may not have been Jewish. This possibility cannot be proven or disproven.

Victor Kugler's second wife, Lucy, had a sister, Rita Visser, living in Mississauga, Ontario, a large suburb west of Toronto. Rita has a photo of Victor Kugler at age five, some school report cards and a picture of him in his navy uniform. But apart from the following significant anecdote regarding the socioenvironmental atmosphere in which he grew up, she has little information regarding his early life. Mrs. Visser revealed that Victor and Lucy were both very private people and did not talk about themselves.

Based on the social history of Sudetenland around the turn of the century, one might surmise that Victor Kugler, being illegitimate, was the object of severe social ostracism in his home territory.

Recent research on the early life of Victor Kugler, revealed in an article in the Anne Frank House magazine, confirmed these assertions, believing that

> young Victor might also have experienced negative reactions, due to being a "bastard." Victor's family was not poor. His mother, who gave him a loving childhood, seems to have died when he was ten years old, as from then on, his report cards were signed by Franz Klose, whose relationship to Victor is unknown. While Victor, for the most part, did well in school, he seems to have lacked the necessary social connections which would have enabled him, with his good academic record, to advance into university and professional circles. Instead, he gravitated towards trade-oriented education. His stigma of illegitimacy could have been the underlying reason for his lack of such social network connections. Victor enrolled at a vocational school for weaving and then he briefly worked as a junior statistician in Berlin before being drafted into the Austrian military during the last years of World War I.

Sudetenland and adjacent northeast Austria was one of the most socially and politically reactionary regions of the entire nineteenth-century German world. As an example of this extreme conservatism, Rita remembers one of the very few anecdotes Victor told her about his early childhood: "When I was young, and we ate, we were not allowed to sit. We had to stand. There was no talking. Children were not allowed to be heard."

Bordering the non-German, Czech, Magyar and Slavic regions, the Sudeten Germans developed a fortress mentality and were particularly susceptible to the influence of Germanic superiority cults, which were popular throughout the late nineteenth century. Hitler himself came from northeast Austria, bordering Sudentenland. The role of the Sudeten Germans in encouraging Hitler's invasion of Czechoslovakia is too familiar to need repeating here.

In such an adverse parochial atmosphere, the young Victor Kugler may well have been a social outcast. It is hypothetical of course, but under the circumstances personal memories of traumatic social ostracism could well explain many important aspects of Victor Kugler's adult personality — the reluctance of this deeply religious Christian to reveal his early life to anybody, his general extreme humility and reticence and his sympathy for Jews, who were the prime object of hostility in the very region where it would have been expressed towards him.

The memoirs of Eda Shapiro, regarding the young adulthood of Victor Kugler, resume:

> At age seventeen, during World War I, he was drafted into the Austrian navy, where he served in the Adriatic. In the navy he worked as an electrician and was wounded.

According to Rita Visser, he served in a submarine in the Adriatic during World War I. She did not know that he was an electrician. Based upon the facts supplied by both Mrs. Visser and Mrs. Shapiro he was, most likely, an electrician in a submarine. Both Mrs. Visser and Mrs. Shapiro agree on the accuracy of the following statement:

> He was discharged after seven months, with a pension, in April 1918.
> The war ended in November 1918.

Otto Frank told Oskar Morawetz in the early 1970s that Victor Kugler had left Austria because he was disgusted with the fascism and anti-Semitism he encountered regularly in the Austrian imperial armed forces during the war. Such a sentiment was extremely rare in rural Sudetenland. Since Victor Kugler had never spent any time in Vienna, Prague, or the other major urban centers where there was a significant Jewish presence, this tends to support the deduction that bitter personal experiences as an illegitimate child might have been the principal reason behind his commendable sympathy for Jewish people, which was to culminate in his hiding the family and friends of Anne Frank.

After the war Victor Kugler left Austria, as Eda Shapiro details:

> He moved to Holland in 1920, and lived in Utrecht for thirteen years. There, he became an employee for a Mr. A., proprietor of a bakery and restaurant which also imported pectin and spices for use in pastry and chocolate. They sold to Germany and Belgium. Victor Kugler traveled in both countries to increase business.
>
> From 1928 to 1933, he managed the office in Utrecht. In 1933, on a business trip to Berlin, he saw Jews being rounded up and marched away to concentration camps. He said:
>
>> In March 1933, I had occasion to visit Germany on business. This was shortly after Hitler took over. Nazi flags were flying from nearly every house. I saw Nazis in brown shirts, with swastikas conspicuously marked on ribbons around their arms, leading away little groups of men. When these prisoners did not move fast enough, they got kicks in the back from the booted Nazis, and the helpless prisoners quickly jumped forward. This was my first impression of Nazism, and I was glad to come back home.
>
> Mr. A. and Victor Kugler decided to consolidate the business in one place: Amsterdam.

Victor Kugler lived in a house in Hilversum, a comfortable Amsterdam suburb. He gained a reputation as an efficient accountant and manager. His main hobby was bird-watching. As he recounted, in 1956, to the now-defunct *Toronto Advertiser*:

> In Holland, I belonged to the Royal Netherlands Bird-watching Association and Hilversum, which is my hometown, is an ideal place for birdwatchers. It's situated in the middle of marshes and lakes and we would often spot ducks from Siberia resting there.

Life for the newly married Victor Kugler settled into a pleasant routine in the Amsterdam suburbs. The first indication that anything was to change happened in 1933, the year Hitler assumed power in Germany. But for now Kugler's life was stable, although the founder of his company, Mr. A., retired, to be replaced by a new owner, Otto Frank, newly relocated from Germany. Victor Kugler continued as manager.

A Brief Summary of the Rise of German Nazism

Eda Shapiro describes the atmosphere of the times:

> In 1921, Adolf Hitler, a frustrated artist and World War I veteran from Austria, became president of the National Socialist German Workers' (Nazi) Party. He was determined to build it into a mass movement and gain control of the country. Hatred of Jews dominated his thinking. Convicted of treason, he wrote *Mein Kampf* in prison. In it he set forth his racial theories and the "final solution of the Jewish problem," i.e., total annihilation of the Jews.
>
> During the 1920s, he built up the Nazi Party. He received financial help from German industries. In the 1930 election (in the throes of the Depression) his party was the second largest. In 1933, Hitler became chancellor (equivalent of prime minister) and in 1934, commander-in-chief of the army. At once he began to rearm Germany to conquer Europe, as he had proposed in *Mein Kampf*. In the storm he unleashed upon Europe, over fifty million were to die.
>
> Jewish communities had existed in Europe for over two thousand years. As countries developed, Jews were rarely given citizenship. They were tolerated as guests at best. Their religious differences made them targets for persecution. This intensified the closeness of Jewish communities. About thirty thousand Jews migrated from Germany to the Netherlands from 1930 on.

The Early Life of Otto Frank

The source for the following information about the early years of Otto Frank is *Anne Frank* by Richard Amdur.

Otto Frank was born in Frankfurt in 1889 (the same year as Hitler). His father, Michael Frank, had founded a banking house named after himself.

Otto got involved in business early in life. In 1909, he dropped out of the prestigious University of Heidelberg to accompany a fellow student, Nathan Straus, to New York. Nathan Straus's family owned Macy's department store. After several trips to New York, where he learned how to run a business on an impromptu, do-it-yourself, crash course basis, Otto worked in Dusseldorf for a few years. During World War I, he and his brother Herbert served in a German artillery regiment where Otto became a lieutenant. Afterwards, he decided to follow in his now-deceased father's footsteps and go into banking, more from a sense of family responsibility than from any authentic interest, as the family bank was now in trouble.

The Frank brothers were too inexperienced to deal with the major problems that were affecting German banking at the time, which were overwhelmingly beyond their control: postwar inflation, the Depression, and, finally, anti-Semitism, which, stirred up by Hitler and Goebbels, constantly loomed just beneath the Weimar Republic's political surface. An unfortunate incident involving Herbert Frank led to an anonymous complaint, tarred with anti-Semitic innuendo, involving one of the bank's financial dealings. This prompted criminal charges and led to Otto Frank's closing the bank for good in March 1933, two months after Hitler took power.

While the 1920s had been a time of bitter business frustration for Otto Frank, they were also the time during which he started his family. In the spring of 1925 he had married Edith Hollander, and less than a year later she gave birth to a daughter, Margot Betti. Four years later, in 1929, their second daughter, Anneliese Marie Frank, was born.

With the bank closed and no further business ties in Germany, Otto Frank realized that Anne and Margot would have no future if the family remained there. Emigration was the only course of action. His choice of destination, Holland, was pretty obvious. He had visited Amsterdam several times on business and was well aware of its tradition of tolerance and reputation as a place of refuge for Jews and others facing discrimination in their home countries.

Luckily, he received a job offer from his brother-in-law, Erich Elias, who had worked with Otto and Herbert Frank in their father's bank but had left Germany in 1929 to open a Swiss branch of Opekta Werke, a subsidiary of the Frankfurt Pomosin Werke. Opekta, a manufacturer and distributor of pectin, a gelling agent used in jams and jellies, wanted to open a retail branch in Amsterdam. Elias offered the position of branch manager to Otto.

As Richard Amdur states in his biography of Anne Frank:

> In the summer of 1933, the Franks left Frankfurt for Aachen, Edith's hometown. Edith, Margot and Anne remained there with Edith's family while Otto went on ahead to Amsterdam to set up the business and find living quarters. A slight hitch in the work arrangements led Otto to set up his own independent food products business using the Opekta trademark, with the help of a loan from his brother-in-law. He then found an apartment at 37 Merwedeplein, a quiet little square in the southern part of the city. Edith and Margot joined Otto in December. Anne arrived in March 1934. The Franks were reunited with Edith's mother (who did not live to go to the Secret Annexe) and ready to begin anew.

The memoirs of Victor Kugler as told to Eda Shapiro pick up from Otto Frank's arrival as follows. The business relationship between Otto and Victor is described in the third person, from Eda's writings:

> Otto's workforce was small at the beginning. He himself was the director. At the beginning of 1935, Mr. A.R.W. Dunselman, an Amsterdam lawyer, was appointed supervisory director. Chief among the few members of his staff was Victor Gustav Kugler.
>
> The most pressing task for the new business was to persuade housewives, mainly in the countryside, to use pectin (which was sold either in small bottles or as a powder in little boxes or paper bags) in jam making. Various kinds of advertising materials were issued. There were several editions of an *Opekta Journal* and advertisements were placed in the press. In 1938 an Opekta film was made to be shown regularly at meetings of housewives' organizations. At the same time, retail outlets, mainly pharmacists, had to be found throughout the country. At first Otto dealt with all these matters in person, but later a woman was taken on to demonstrate at housewives' meetings.

Anne Frank Prior to the Secret Annex

Eda relates, in Victor's words, his meeting with the young girl whose story was to become inextricably linked with his own:

I first saw Anne Frank when she was only four years old, in March 1934. Mrs. Frank had come to the office to visit her husband, and it was the first time she had brought the children with her. I was introduced to Margot and Anne and I recall that they took a few minutes to size me up. They must have decided that I was "OK" because soon the three of us were engaged in a lively conversation.

Already, at that tender age, there was a marked difference in the temperament of the two girls. Margot, the older one, stood calmly and looked around the room. Anne, on the other hand, was much more lively and personally investigated whatever interested her. Even in those early minutes of our acquaintance I was struck by her large, dark brown eyes; those probing, searching, questioning eyes.

When Anne was still in kindergarten and school hours permitted, Mrs. Frank often brought her downtown to the office. The child would be delighted to see her father and Mr. Frank would be equally pleased to see his small daughter. She always brought a welcome interruption with her pleasant chatter.

One of the schools Anne attended was the Montessori School, which she liked very much. I thought she was quite intelligent and in general more developed mentally than most children her age or even older, Anne was not a brilliant student. Perhaps this was because her mind was always full of ideas not necessarily connected with the lesson of the moment. Perhaps the budding writer was already stirring within her.

As Margot and Anne grew older, the different traits in their characters became more noticeable. However, each time I visited the Franks it struck me how alike the girls were when it came to kindness and courtesy, qualities which neither of them ever lacked. Anne's emotions ran the full gamut. As she says in her diary, "They haven't given me the name 'little bundle of contradictions' all for nothing!"

Generally, Anne was a talkative young lady. This characteristic often manifested itself at school. As a consequence, one punishment she received was to write an essay entitled "Chatterbox." Obviously this punishment didn't work, for it was soon followed by a second assignment, entitled "Incurable Chatterbox." Most of the time, Anne was cheerful, friendly, and brimming over with fun and laughter.

The Evian Conference

Eda Shapiro describes the West's shrugging off of responsibility for the events in Europe that would determine the fate of that bright-eyed girl:

> In July 1938, US President Franklin Delano Roosevelt initiated the Evian Conference of the Western countries in France. No country (including the United States and Canada) wanted the peaceful, cultured, industrious Jews. So until May 1945, Jews were in a no-man's-land, trapped. Gypsies were also marginalized.

The organized, nationwide German pogrom known as Kristallnacht, which was the beginning of the Holocaust, took place four months later on the night of November 9-10, 1938.

Holland before 1940

Anton Mussert's Dutch National Socialist Party, NSB, founded in 1931, was supported by only 5 percent of the population, but after 1940, that 5 percent became a fifth column. They helped and imitated the German Nazis.

Even before the German conquest of Holland, Victor Kugler experienced unpleasant encounters with these nascent Dutch Nazis because he worked with Otto Frank, a Jew. According to a 1970 interview with Ron Poulton of the *Toronto Telegram*:

> In November 1939, we had a visit from a real Nazi. He had a cigarette in his mouth, and when I told him I had been in the Austrian navy, he took it out and said: "Oh, that's all for today." But Mr. Frank was a Jew and things got worse for them.

Holland under German Rule

Indeed, life was drastically changed under the Nazi regime, as Eda Shapiro describes:

> At the end of May 1940, SS General Artur Seyss-Inquart became Reichskommissar of the Netherlands. Although he promised basic rights, the government was soon dissolved and only the Nazi party remained. Politicians and leaders were sent to concentration camps. Dictatorial laws and laws prescribing discrimination against Jews were enforced. Seyss-Inquart was tried and hanged in Nuremburg shortly after the war. In his book, *Four Years in the Netherlands,* he wrote: "The Jews are not Dutchmen. They're enemies with whom we can conclude no armistice and no peace. Do not expect from me an order which lays this down, apart from police regulations. We will strike the Jews where we meet them, and he who goes with them has to bear the consequences. The Führer has declared that the role of the Jews in Europe has come to an end, and therefore so it has." Thus out of 140,000 Jews, only thirty-five thousand survived.
>
> The first decrees against the Jews of Holland came in February 1941. Shopkeepers and craftsmen in a Jewish district in Amsterdam were molested by Dutch Nazis. The Germans did not intervene. But the Dutch people did. The plight of the Jews was growing worse daily, and anti-Semitic decrees were following one another quickly. They prohibited Jews from restaurants, theaters, cinemas, streetcars and other transportation such as trains. Jews were not even allowed to drive their own cars. Then came decrees prohibiting Jews from swimming pools, tennis courts, hockey fields and other sports grounds. Then a curfew was imposed for them to be indoors by eight P.M. Shopping was allowed only between three and five P.M., in stores marked "Jewish Shop." Jews were forbidden to visit Christians and could only attend Jewish schools. They were even forced to hand in their bicycles [*then and even now the major form of inner-city transportation in the Netherlands — ed.*].
>
> On February 25 and 26, 1941, all the people of Amsterdam rose up, demonstrating their friendship for the Jews, and went on strike.

The dock workers went further, entering the Jewish districts to help in any way they could.

Today, a monument in Amsterdam commemorates this demonstration. It is a statue of a dock worker, an appreciation by the Jewish people of their Dutch friends, and it stands on the square before the main synagogue. After two days, the strike was easily broken by reinforced German police who arrested many people, especially union leaders and politicians. Other strikes followed in other cities in Holland.

A sharp decree was issued by the top SS leaders. It warned that any future strikers would be severely punished. Property would be confiscated and prison terms and even death would await them. All of this actually stiffened resistance against the Germans.

The Dutch Underground movement grew more active. It distributed leaflets with messages from the Dutch government in England, and forwarded information about the Germans that could be useful to the Allies.

In May 1941, Germany's infamous Nuremberg Laws were introduced into the Netherlands. All Jews received personal identification cards, with photographs and fingerprints and a big "J" stamped on them. All public officials had to declare they were not of Jewish origin. Any who were suffered dismissal.

Then all Jews were forced to wear a yellow six-pointed star (Magen David) with the inscription "JOOD" (Jew), to distinguish them from non-Jews. The Dutch people became more sympathetic. Later, the Jews had to be registered by the "Joodenraad" (Jewish Council). This made it easy for the Nazis to round them up. The next step was deportation.

Reaction by Otto Frank

Victor Kugler gave Eda Shapiro a window into Otto Frank's thinking at the time:

> After Hitler's rise to power in Germany in 1933, Otto Frank, Anne's father, moved his family to Amsterdam. By 1940, when he realized

that the anti-Semitic pattern in Germany was beginning to repeat itself in Holland, he felt he had to take further steps in order to protect his family. A plan was taking shape in his mind — to prepare a place of refuge.

When events and time dictated, Otto Frank and his family would go into hiding.

It arrived earlier than expected.

Early in July 1942 Margot Frank received an official letter with an ornate Nazi-swastika masthead, ordering her to report for deportation to Germany within a few days.

Chapter Four

The Secret Annex

And so began, as Victor Kugler would later call it, "the Story." Eda Shapiro gives us Victor Kugler's words:

"The time has come for us to hide."

These words are still ringing in my ears, though I heard them back on July 6, 1942. They were spoken by Otto Frank, father of Anne Frank, who will eternally be remembered through the book *The Diary of Anne Frank*.

My name is Victor Kugler. I am the "Mr. Kraler" of Anne's diary.

"The Germans have ordered Margot to report to a collection point, from where they plan to ship her to Germany," Mr. Frank continued. "We must use our 'Secret Annex' sooner than anticipated."

Margot was Anne's sixteen-year-old sister.

Anne Frank was a lively adolescent. Margot was a lovely girl, too, studious and more subdued. The Franks all had many friends. Their life in Holland was satisfying and pleasant — until the Nazis came into the picture.

The offices and warehouse of both of Otto Frank's firms were housed in an old four-story house, 263 Prinsengracht, near the famous Wester Church where Rembrandt is buried. Now this building was chosen for yet another purpose. It was to serve as the hiding place for the Frank family and four other people.

The upper rear two floors of the house were separated from the main part by a staircase. We were able to conceal its very existence by building a movable bookcase across the door which led to it. The quarters beyond it contained several rooms, a toilet and a sink.

For over a year, we had been stocking the secret hiding place with food, bedding and essential furniture. I had been working with Mr. Frank since 1933. Now I took over the firm, where I had previously been employed as general manager. Mr. Frank asked me to continue in that capacity. My wife and I had become good friends with his family. Mr. Frank was an educated man who was proud of his Jewish heritage. Mrs. Frank was a religious woman and a devoted mother and wife.

Besides Mr. Kleiman and myself, only two of Mr. Frank's other employees were aware of our planned hiding place. These were the two office girls, Miep and Elli. Mr. Kleiman and I assumed ostensible ownership of the two firms that belonged to Mr. Frank. Had we not done this, the Germans would have confiscated Mr. Frank's property because he was a Jew.

According to Ernst Schnabel's initial historical account, which was published in 1958, a "planning session" between Otto Frank, Victor Kugler and Jo Kleiman was held to formally implement this ostensible change of ownership in March 1942. Victor Kugler's narrative continues:

A few weeks before the Frank family went into hiding, Anne had celebrated her thirteenth birthday: June 12, 1942. She brought with her a beloved gift from that occasion, a diary.

Before the Franks went into hiding we planted several clues to indicate that they had left the country. A letter written by Mr. Frank was reposted from a border town. Also, my wife and I were invited to a dinner at the Franks' home; we hoped the neighbors would inter-pret this as a "farewell." My wife was in poor health, and, not wishing to worry her, I did not tell her of the Secret Annex plans. Anne was a talkative young lady but during that particular dinner she was strangely silent. In a general lull in the conversation, she gazed into my wife's eyes, and after a moment said: "I have just spoken to Mrs. Kugler and she has not heard."

That fateful day in July 1942, when the Frank family decided to go into hiding, was uncomfortably hot and muggy. One by one, the members of the family disappeared into the Secret Annex. They looked a sorry lot, for they were wearing layer upon layer of clothing. To avoid suspicion they carried only small parcels. As Anne said in her diary: "I had on two vests, two pair of knickers, a dress; on top of that a skirt, jacket, summer coat, two pairs stockings, shoes, and more. I was nearly stifled before we started, but no one inquired of me about that."

A week after the Frank family "disappeared" into their hiding place, they were joined by Mr. van Pels (van Daan in the *diary*), his wife and their son, fifteen-year-old Peter. A little later they made room for yet another person, Friedrich Pfeffer (Albert Dussel in the *diary*), a refugee dentist.

From the day they entered the Secret Annex, these people's lives changed completely. They were literally cut off from the outside world. The four walls and roof were the boundaries of their existence. All the windows had to be curtained, blacked out and shuttered. They had to make sure that they were neither seen nor heard, particularly in the daytime. And always there was the fear of being discovered. They were forced to live in close proximity with one another. They had to endure trying situations and often irritating behavior.

Life inside the Secret Annex, with all its frustrations and tensions, has been fully described by Anne Frank in her diary. In this book, the talented young girl reported the trials and tribulations and even humorous incidents. With unusual insight and perception, she recorded her feelings, ambitions, and philosophy of life. That she was wise beyond her years, the diary attests; that her memory will live on is assured.

Those of us on the outside who shared the secret were also subject to a great deal of anxiety and tension. Our greatest fear was that the hiding place might be discovered. I had to put on a good "act" for Mr. Frank's former business associates, customers and neighbors. Many other Jewish families in Holland tried to hide in factories, warehouses, etc. If these unfortunate people forgot to draw the shades — if their faces were seen just once at the windows — that would be enough to betray their secret, and they were no longer safe. Indeed, they were doomed.

Toronto's Holy Blossom Temple is Canada's leading Reform Jewish synagogue. Its most famous rabbi, Rabbi W. Gunther Plaut, was himself a German-Jewish refugee from Hitler. More than a decade before he met Eda Shapiro, Victor Kugler revealed further details concerning the period of the Secret Annex in the April 1958 Holy Blossom Temple Brotherhood periodical:

> We, my friend and I, and also two girls of the office [*Miep Gies and Elli Vossens*] went every day upstairs to have a talk with them [*the Franks, van Pelses and others sheltered by Otto Frank*] and to ask what they needed so they could care for it: not only for the daily food that was rationed and we had every month to buy ration cards in the black market, but also for other things that made living for them more comfortable and pretty. They had also a radio, although it was strictly forbidden to have one. We listened every day to the transmissions of the BBC and of the Dutch Free Radio in London, England.
>
> We followed the progressions of the Allied armies and when the message of the landing in France came through (D-Day, June 6, 1944), everyone was in a high spirit. Now it could not take any more a long time till the ultimate liberation. Our visits in the noon and after office hours broke the monotony for the locked-up people.
>
> When their nerves got stressed and some small quarrel raised, we could break the tension and all things were fine again.

Victor also revealed in the Brotherhood periodical further impressions of Anne Frank's diary as she wrote her entries, day by day:

> She considered it as her friend and entered, every day, her impressions about the people and other facts up there. She had for her age of thirteen years a very clever spirit. She was able to express her thoughts in such fine words and sentences that later, when the diary was found, nobody could believe that a girl of thirteen could have written it. Besides that, she was full of jokes and people could often laugh. Sometimes her jokes had a deeper human sense and were not always readily understood.

Hamilton, Ontario, Canada's steel city, is situated on Lake Ontario, forty miles west of Toronto and fifty miles northwest of Buffalo, New York. In

March 1974, Victor Kugler was interviewed by its daily newspaper, *the Spectator*. He told of a special recollection of Anne:

> Anne had quite big eyes and I remember once, when she had a birthday, how those eyes lit up when I gave her a book.

In this article, Kugler also remembered how

> Anne used to enjoy reading Dickens and she would get excited listening to the voice of Winston Churchill coming over the radio from London.

The March 23, 1974, *Spectator* article goes on to say:

> Frequently when Mr. Kugler visited the annex, Anne was writing in her beloved diary, a small red-checkered cloth-covered book which had been given to her on her thirteenth birthday.
>
> For more than two years, the young Jewish girl confided in her diary all the thoughts she had been unable to share with another human being.

Paul Kidd's *Spectator* article underscored Anne's very special confidence in Victor Kugler as her ultimate protector:

> At her first entry in the diary on June 12, 1942 (before she went into hiding), the young Jewish girl wrote: "I hope I shall be able to confide in you completely, as I have never been able to do in anyone before, and I hope that you will be a great support and comfort to me."

Elli visited Toronto in 1978, when Oskar Morawetz's symphonic work *From the Diary of Anne Frank* was premiered, of which more later. While she was in Toronto, she made a reel-to-reel tape of her recollections of the Secret Annex period. This tape is still in Mr. Morawetz's possession. She spoke in Dutch and Victor Kugler and his second wife Lucy translated her words into English on the same tape.

Elli recounted the terrible tensions in the Secret Annex, from the periodic chiming of the church bells, to the constant need for silence at all hours of the day and night when there was even the slightest chance of being discovered. She wondered how anybody could live in such a place, under such constant tension, and not go quickly insane. Victor Kugler added:

We therefore had strict regulations. The occupants of the Secret Annex could not wear shoes or flush the toilet in the daytime because we had workmen downstairs. Also, I told them to keep the window shades drawn at all times, and never to show their faces at a window, lest they be seen.

Anne, sensitive and perceptive as she was, obviously understood my anxiety. When I read the diary, I was much moved by this passage:

> Miep and Kraler (myself) carry the heaviest burden of the eight in hiding. Miep in all she does and Kraler through the enormous responsibility, which is sometimes so much for him that he can hardly talk from pent-up nerves and strain.

However, in spite of anxiety and tension, life went on both inside and outside the Secret Annex. Every week, I would bring a magazine. Anne especially liked *Cinema and Theater Magazine Illustrated*. She would cut out the pictures and paste them on the wall. This was the only magazine Hitler allowed.

Every time I brought it for her, Anne would look at me, and her eyes seemed to say: "Did you bring me *Cinema and Theater*? You know how much I enjoy it." I would hide it in my pocket, so that I could watch those questioning eyes for longer.

Sometimes, as I went about my daily chores, I found it hard to believe that a little over two years had passed since the Franks and their friends had gone into hiding.

Their only hope for a better future was their secret hiding place. In this annex they hoped to "ride out the storm" and emerge once more as free human beings.

The Franks' Lifeline

Richard Amdur, in his book *Anne Frank*, describes the location of the building that served as home for the Franks and their friends for twenty-five long months:

> The backyard building that housed the Secret Annex was built in

1635 and was near the Prinsengracht, one of the main canals in a city
famous for its canals. On one side was another building filled with
offices. On the other was a furniture workshop. The ground floor
served as a warehouse. The first floor and the front part of the second
floor served as office and storage space for Otto Frank's food-prod-
ucts business. During the day, Miep, Mr. Kleiman, Elli Vossens, and
other employees worked in the large, light front office while Mr.
Kugler occupied the rear office. Prior to his "disappearance,"
Hermann van Pels had shared this space with Kugler.

This business — and its new owner, Victor Kugler — served as a lifeline for
the people in hiding in the Secret Annex.

Evelyn Wolfe is a Toronto-born woman who befriended Victor and Lucy
Kugler after they immigrated to Toronto. This friendship will be described in
greater detail in chapter 8. Eda Wolfe told me several other revealing things
Victor had told her about his life during the Secret Annex period.

Foremost was the fact that Victor Kugler, as Otto Frank's managing partner, kept the Franks' business going. Elli and Miep were the office girls, but it
fell to Victor Kugler to sustain both the spice business and the Secret Annex.
Miep and Elli, invaluable as their contribution was, were only in their early
twenties. They could not have done it on their own. Victor Kugler, in his
forties, possessed the maturity, business acumen and street smarts essential
for supervising and maintaining the remarkably smooth operation of the
Secret Annex.

If it had not been for him, the Franks and van Pelses and Dr. Pfeffer would
have starved within a month. Not only did Victor earn the business income to
sustain them, he also personally organized the purchase of their food (with
the cooperation of Henk and Miep Gies and others who obtained forged
ration cards via the Dutch Underground).

Canadian composer Oskar Morawetz, about whom more will be said
later, and who also became a friend of Victor Kugler's in Canada, remarks that
the purchase of the food ration coupons, which Mr. Kugler coordinated, was
a very tricky and often tense bureaucratic process.

The difficulty of obtaining food during the German occupation of the
Netherlands, even for average Dutch Christians who were not being directly
persecuted by the Nazi occupiers, is underscored by Victor Kugler's sister-in-

law, Rita Visser. She was a very young girl in Amsterdam during the war, but she remembered her own family's experiences during this trying period:

> We don't know how Victor got the food for the Franks *and the others*, because my family in Amsterdam was constantly begging during the war. We often had to walk for two weeks at a time, just to obtain food. We had to take the ferry, which was north of Amsterdam. The Germans would be waiting at the ferry docks and if they found out that we had food, they would take it all.

The bottom line, Rita Visser said, was that food could only be bought on the black market. Victor Kugler conducted all of this activity under the most clandestine conditions, which was especially difficult during the summer when complete darkness does not descend upon Holland until 10:30 P.M. He could only deliver the provisions under cover of darkness. As if this *were* not enough, he bought Anne Frank the Hollywood magazines she loved. He also managed to buy all kinds of other supplies, ranging from schoolbooks to household odds and ends. He told Evelyn Wolfe:

> We got a correspondence course in Latin for Margot, while they were hiding, and her teacher wrote that she had never had such a bright pupil!

Clearly, he was assuming great risks. In one of his taped interviews, Evelyn Wolfe asked, "Why did you stick your neck out?" He replied: "I had to. They were my friends." He summed up his underlying sentiments from the Secret Annex period: "We helped each other as much as we could. What we could do, we did."

In July 1970, Ron Poulton, a columnist for one of North America's most legendary and colorful newspapers, the *Toronto Telegram*, wrote up a lengthy interview with Victor Kugler at age seventy. In it, Mr. Kugler filled in some more details of the Secret Annex period:

> A Dutch Nazi living in Hamburg was our main competitor and he knew Mr. Frank was a Jew. One day he came to us and ordered us to open our books, but Mr. Frank was already hiding in the house. One morning, before the traffic was heavy, Mr. Frank and his family had walked to it (the warehouse which housed the Secret Annex), wearing several layers of clothing. Their house was forty minutes away from Prinsengracht.

According to the Poulton article, Kugler and his partner from Hilversum, a southeastern suburb of Amsterdam, moved the Franks into the Secret Annex. Anne later called the partner "Mr. Koophuis" (his real name was Johannes Kleiman) and Kugler "Mr. Kraler," because real names were never used by the Dutch Underground. However, according to the Evelyn Wolfe tape, Victor Kugler legally changed his name to Victor Kraler in order to conceal his Austrian-German ancestry, because there was increasing anti-German sentiment in the Dutch population as the war and the brutal German occupation dragged on. In addition to the Kraler name, Victor Kugler told Evelyn Wolfe he had other names as well.

The Security Role of Victor Kugler

Both Anne's diary and Miep Gies's memoirs, *Anne Frank Remembered*, relate that Victor Kugler was the one who had a bookcase hinged in front of the door to the Secret Annex. Anne Frank, in her diary entry of August 21, names the man who made the bookcase, a Mr. Voskuijl, whom she identifies as another workman who was let into the secret and whose help was invaluable.

According to Miep Gies, the man who actually hinged the bookcase was Hans Vossen, the father of the other office girl, Elli Vossen. (Was Voskuijl a pseudonym for Hans Vossen? We may never know one way or another. But in the final analysis, the answer to this question does not matter. What does matter is the fact that the bookcase was constructed and placed in its vital security position by an employee, or employees, of Victor Kugler's.)

According to Miep Gies, Elli asked Victor Kugler if her unemployed father, who had five other children, could find work at 263 Prinsengracht. Kugler discussed the matter with Otto Frank, who was still the real *decision maker*. Otto Frank consented to the request. Hans Vossen's job was to mix spices, pack and ship them. He took his orders from Victor Kugler.

Still, for all of these security preparations, the Franks and their companions lived in constant fear of being discovered by the Germans and their Dutch collaborators. According to Rita Visser, Anne thought it was very scary to go into Victor's back office.

Yet for over two years, the Secret Annex remained undiscovered.

Betrayal

This setup would have continued on a self-sustaining basis until the Allied liberation of Holland, which took place on May 7, 1945, if there had not been a betrayal to the Gestapo. Who was the betrayer? According to the diary, it was most likely a thief who broke into the building on Easter Sunday 1944, was confronted by the Franks with a flashlight, and then informed the police.

But Rita Visser has more detailed and specific suspicions. She reports that on July 16, 1943, burglars broke into the building. But she suspected warehouse foreman Willem van Maaren of having betrayed the people in hiding in the Secret Annex. According to Mrs. Visser:

> J.J. de Kok, who worked for a short time as van Maaren's assistant in the warehouse, claimed to have known nothing about the people in hiding. But he did know that van Maaren sometimes stole things and even assisted in several thefts at Prinsengracht 263.
>
> After the war, in response to these accusations, Otto Frank said, "Let it go." However, in 1957, Victor Kugler wrote in a letter to a journalist that he suspected van Maaren of having a role in the betrayal.

There was a follow-up to these suspicions, including the utilization of possible evidence implicating van Maaren. But, probably in accordance with Otto Frank's wishes to "let it go," nothing decisive ever came of it.

In the diary and its popular theatrical version, Victor, as Mr. Kraler, mentions to the Franks a "Karl" who might or might not have been involved. But there is no evidence that such a Karl actually existed. More recent research points to Lena van Bladeren Hartog, a cleaning lady who occasionally worked at Prinsengracht 263.

Perhaps the most convincing theory as to who the betrayer could have been was proposed during the summer of 2002, fifty years after the Franks went into hiding, when British author Carol Ann Lee's biography, *The Hidden Life of Otto Frank*, was published. According to Noah Freedman of Toronto's *Jewish Standard*, Lee argued that the real culprit was Tony Ahlers, a business associate who was also a petty thief and an avowed anti-Semite.

Freedman, in the October 2002 issue of the *Jewish Standard*, writes that Ahlers had a letter in his possession, written by a former Opekta employee, accusing Frank of making "anti-German comments." Lee argues that Frank paid Ahlers to keep quiet about it.

Freedman goes on to say:

> But Ahlers, Lee maintains, had few principles and never believed that "a deal was a deal." One of the Dutch policemen who participated in the raid on Prinsengracht was Martin Kuiper, a friend of Ahlers'. Moreover, after the war The Hague convicted Ahlers of betrayal and jailed him for his wartime activities.
>
> Carol Ann Lee has at least one supporter of her thesis. Shortly after the release of her book she received a call from Tony Ahlers' son. He told her in clear and unequivocal terms that "My father did not 'probably' betray Otto Frank and his family. He most certainly did. I have no doubt about that."

Regardless of who the betrayer was, there is no doubt that a betrayal did take place, as the Gestapo, on August 4, 1944, went straight to the Secret Annex without any hit-or-miss preliminary investigation.

Chapter Five

Arrest, Incarceration and Deportation

Eda Shapiro records Victor Kugler's recounting of the bitter end of the Secret Annex:

> On that fateful Friday (August 4, 1944), while I was working in my office, I heard an unusual commotion. It sounded as if several people were running up and down the *first-floor* corridor. I opened my office door and saw four policemen. One was a uniformed Gestapo man. The other three were Dutch. One of the Dutch policemen was a Maarten van R., a notorious collaborator who was executed after the liberation. The Gestapo man was an Austrian named Karl Silberbauer and he was obviously in charge.
>
> "Who's the owner of this building?" he snapped.
>
> I gave him the name and address of the owner since, indeed, we did not own the property on 263 Prinsengracht. We only rented it.

According to the Evelyn Wolfe interview tape, Victor Kugler stated that the Gestapo wanted him to say that the business still belonged to Mr. Frank and that he was just a "straw man" serving as a front. If he had done so, the Gestapo would have immediately confiscated the business for themselves. He said on the tape that when he was asked by the Gestapo if Otto Frank in any way still owned the business, he replied no.

Mr. Kugler's memoirs as told to Eda Shapiro continue:

> "No, no!" he said impatiently. "I want to know who is responsible here?"
>
> "I am," I replied.

"Now," Silberbauer ordered, "show us the rooms in the building."

I started with my office, and to appear cooperative, I opened all the bookcases and cabinets for his inspection. Next I led him to the back of the building and showed him the office of the "Travies Company," where Mr. Kleiman worked. I even showed him the washroom and our little kitchen.

Outwardly I showed great calm, but inwardly I was terrified. I wondered why these men were here. Had they found out that I had been taking pictures for the Dutch Underground? Or were they searching for the secret hiding place? Had we been betrayed?

Silberbauer ordered me up to the next floor. He followed me and after him came the other three policemen. First I went to the stockroom in the first part of the building. His three helpers stayed behind, in the corridor.

"Now," said Silberbauer, "let's look for secret weapons."

Next we went to the corridor in the back and my heart was in my mouth. We had come to the crucial place. The bookcase that concealed the entrance to the Secret Annex was in this area.

Next to this bookcase, along the side wall, there was a similar bookcase and some boxes. I noticed that this bookcase and the boxes had been moved from their original place. Obviously it was the work of the three Dutch policemen. To my horror I now saw these same men tampering with the bookcase that hid the entrance to the Secret Annex.

However, the bookcase did not yield an inch. Again and again they tried to move it but they failed. Finally, they found the hook that kept it in its place. The hook was unfastened and they moved the bookcase. The door leading to the staircase and rooms above was now exposed.

My heart sank.

The moment I had been dreading for two years had now arrived.

I realized the object of this search. I knew we had been betrayed. The secret had been revealed and our plans had failed. The eight people in the Secret Annex were now doomed. A terrible fate awaited them all.

The Secret Annex Exposed

One of the policemen took a gun (a flat Browning) out of his jacket, and ordered me up the stairs. The other three followed me with their guns drawn.

The first person I saw was Mrs. Frank, sitting motionless in the living room. I whispered "Gestapo" as I entered, but she did not move. Now the dreaded moment had arrived, she seemed stunned. The others came slowly from the other room, and down from the top floor. The only sign of emotion was from Margot, who was weeping silently.

"All right," said Silberbauer. "Get your things together." The Gestapo usually allowed only a few minutes for the gathering of personal belongings. However, a strange incident took place. Silberbauer's eyes were riveted on a grey chest with iron hinges.

"Who claims ownership of this chest?" he shouted. "How did you get it?" "This chest belongs to me!" said Mr. Frank. "I was an officer in the *German army* in World War One." That was perfectly true. Otto Frank had been drafted after high school. He had served in artillery at the Somme, and had been one of those unusual officers commissioned in the field.

Silberbauer's face turned scarlet. A Jewish officer in the German army? He was dumbfounded. Almost angrily, he demanded, "Then why didn't you give yourself up and register?" Mr. Frank did not answer. Silberbauer continued, "You would have been sent to Theresienstadt!" [*While Theresienstadt was ostensibly meant to be a camp for the privileged, in point of fact, its death rate was very high and for many it was just a way station to Auschwitz-Birkenau. — ed.*]

I watched the Nazi Silberbauer struggling with his mixed feelings. I was wondering which would be stronger: his drilled-in respect for officers or his sense of duty?

How ironic that Theresienstadt was named after the Empress Maria Theresa Hapsburg, the subject of the book I had given Anne Frank on her fifteenth birthday. Her diary entry of June 13, 1944, reads: "Another birthday has gone by, so I'm fifteen. I received quite a lot of presents…and the high spot of all, the book *Maria Theresa* and three slices of full-cream cheese from Kraler."

Now, scarcely two months after Anne's fifteenth birthday, Karl Silberbauer had come to attention in front of Mr. Frank and one had the feeling that a sharp command would make him salute.

Since Mr. Frank continued to be silent, Silberbauer finally said: "All right. Get your things together. You can take your time."

The police looked on as the eight inhabitants of the Secret Annex silently gathered their belongings. The Frank family and the other four unfortunate human beings spoke not a word. However, their expressions were most revealing. Their faces registered fear and their knowledge of the harsh fate that awaited them.

Finally, Silberbauer ordered them to go downstairs with their luggage. Mr. Kleiman and I were ordered to go along as well. We were told to go to the warehouse and through the door leading outside, where a little police car was waiting.

As we passed through the warehouse we saw the two men who worked there. We later suspected that one of them had called the police and had revealed the secret hiding place.

We were ordered into the police car and brought to the Gestapo headquarters on Euterpe Street. Mr. Kleiman and myself were now taken to a cell. At a distance, in the corridor outside Silberbauer's office, we saw the Franks, the van Pelses and Friedrich Pfeffer. All eight looked serious and troubled, not knowing what the future would bring. We waved to each other, and that was goodbye. Otto Frank was the only one we ever saw again.

Mitgefangen, Mitgehangen

"*Mitgefangen, mitgehangen* (Caught with them, you will be hanged with them)." With these words, Silberbauer addressed Mr. Kleiman and me when he called us for our first interrogation. This took place in a barred room in the prison itself. Silberbauer leaned back in his chair, lit a cigarette and proceeded to interrogate us.

As I sat in this dreary room I recognized some familiar objects: Peter van Pels's new bicycle, the one he got a short time before he and his family went into hiding; a small roll of gold coins belonging to Friedrich Pfeffer; and a number of objects that were the property of Mr. Frank. I felt a great pang when I looked at these inanimate objects that had belonged to my friends. They bore mute witness to the tragic fate that had overtaken all of us. The interrogation began. "Where were you born?" Silberbauer asked me.

I answered proudly, "Austria," and followed it up by saying, "I served in the Austrian navy in the First World War." I particularly emphasized that, because from his dialect I noticed that he himself was an Austrian. Maybe the shock was too great for him. First, Mr. Frank — a Jew — an officer in the German army, and now, somebody from the Austrian *navy*. He leaned forward, put out his cigarette, and stopped further interrogation with the words, "That's enough for today."

A plainclothesman came in and led Mr. Kleiman and myself to cells in the basement. In a few hours we were transferred to the official prison on the Amstelveenseweg. They crowded six prisoners into cells meant for one.

A few weeks later, one of these prisoners, an old man, was taken away for questioning. He had been caught listening to the radio. The Germans had ordered that all radios be turned over to them. When the old man returned to our cell after the interrogation, he placed his arms on a table, lowered his head on them, and wept bitterly. We, the prisoners, finally managed to calm him and learned that he had witnessed the torture of Jews (as well as Gentiles who were accused of hiding Jews). He had seen a professional boxer hitting them. And he had heard their anguished cries as they were subjected to the terrible thumb screw torture (an instrument of torture consisting of compressing the thumb by turning a screw). It was, therefore, with some fear that I went to Silberbauer's office for my next questioning, along with Kleiman.

Again, the interrogation was short.

My next move was to a prison in another part of town. Here I was put into a private cell, where the luxury astonished me. The walls were painted and the cell contained a bed. On the bed was a pillow, clean sheets and blankets. There was even a bright electric light in the ceiling. I sat down on the bed in order to get better acquainted with my new surroundings. Soon I discovered some pitiful messages scratched on the walls: "I too will be shot. Pray for me." "I die for the queen and our Fatherland. God is with me."

It became clear to me that I was in a cell reserved for those who had been sentenced to death for actions aiding the enemy. I broke into a cold sweat, for I was sure that my last hours had come. After a short while, which seemed like an eternity to me, a German guard opened the door and harshly demanded, "What are you doing here?"

I answered, "I was brought here."

"Get out!" he shouted. "You don't belong here."

I was thankful to leave this terror-filled cell, where many prisoners before me had grimly awaited the hour of their execution.

The guard took me to another crowded cell where I found my friend, Mr. Kleiman.

I had been placed in cell B 3-11 and Mr. Kleiman occupied the next cell. Every day we were sent outside for a period, to take exercise in a heavily guarded court. During these periods, Mr. Kleiman and I had an arrangement whereby he was the last man to leave his cell and I was the first to leave mine.

We walked very close together and exchanged little pieces of paper with messages on them. There was quite a turnover of occupants in those cells, and every new prisoner brought fresh tidings from the outside, so that we were quite well informed as to what was happening outside our prison walls.

An Old Acquaintance

One day the door of my cell was opened and a new prisoner was pushed in. The man kept staring at me, without saying a word. I found it highly annoying and I finally asked him, "Do you mind telling me why you keep staring at me?"

The man gave a penetrating look and said, "You are from Utrecht, are you not?"

That question surprised me. I said, "Before moving to Amsterdam, I lived in Utrecht for thirteen years, but I don't recall ever having seen you."

His face brightened and he said: "You see, I am right. I did see you in Utrecht; many times in fact. It was some years ago, and at the time, I was a policeman. I was directing traffic at the corner of Vradenburg and Lange Viestraat, and many times I saw you crossing that particular corner. My last position was chief of the police station in the *Rode Brug* (Red Bridge) district."

I knew that neighborhood and I also confirmed that during the years between 1928 and 1933 I did, indeed, cross at the special corner he mentioned several times a day. I asked, "How long have you been imprisoned, and why did the Germans pick you up?"

Mr. De H. (that was the gentleman's name) answered that he had been a prisoner for two years now, during which time he had been pushed around from prison to prison. In his function as chief of a police station, he had been ordered by the Germans to bring a transport of Jews to Amsterdam. That was in 1942. He refused, and was imprisoned. Since then, he had not heard anything of his wife and son. All he knew was that his house had been evacuated and that nothing was left of his belongings.

There is an interesting epilogue to Mr. De H.'s story.

After the liberation I went to Utrecht and tried to find out what had happened to him. I checked with the head office of the Utrecht police department. I asked if De H. had been freed and if he was perhaps back in the Red Bridge district. To my delight, I was told that he had been set free and was back in his former position, as chief of police.

I went to see Mr. De H. He was very pleased to see me and told me the following remarkable story.

Towards the end of 1944, two *drunken* German soldiers fell into a canal in Utrecht. A couple of Dutch policemen fished them out and saved their lives. This incident made a terrific impression on the

Germans in Utrecht, and they said to the policemen, "What can we do for you in appreciation?"

The policemen asked for time to think it over.

Shortly afterwards, they requested that Mr. De H. be set free. The Germans in Utrecht couldn't give immediate consent to this request. They had to refer it to higher authorities. But after a couple of months, the request was granted and Mr. De H. was set free.

I was so glad that Mr. De H.'s story had a happy ending. It was most fitting that this man of valor — this man who risked everything in order to save his fellow human beings — was now free, back in his former position, and best of all, reunited with his wife and son.

The Moment of Truth

It was Monday, September 4, 1944, past eight P.M., the curfew hour for the citizens of Amsterdam. In the stilled city, frightened human eyes peered furtively from behind closed windows. Fingers were pointing at the strange scene taking place on the street outside. Streetcars were passing by, transporting prisoners from the Amstelveensweg prison. German soldiers with automatic rifles on their laps were riding in automobiles alongside the streetcars. Mr. Kleiman and I were among these prisoners. Our destination was the Huis van Bewaring (the "House of Custody"). Prisoners were kept here, on the Weteringschans, in Amsterdam, while awaiting trial.

The next morning there was a roll call and a number of men were picked out. I was among them. I suppose I was picked because I looked healthy and strong enough for the work they had in mind. We had to get into brown prison clothes and were brought by truck to a plant on Valckeniers Street.

Our job was to dismantle machines for shipment to Germany. The Germans got replacements for the bombed-out plants in their own country by stealing from the occupied countries. At five P.M., a bell rang and there was a roll call. Two prisoners were missing, and the Germans were furious. In spite of an extensive search, the two prisoners could not be found, and we were finally taken back to prison.

The following morning, we went back to work in the same plant. In the evening two more men were missing. The Germans went wild with rage. They took up their rifles and were ready to kill two prisoners at random. One of the soldiers stood very close to me and I could look straight into the barrel of his rifle. It was not pleasant. We all waited and there was a deadly silence.

Suddenly, someone called, "There they are!" and indeed two men came slowly along.

"Where the hell were you?" the commanding officer bellowed. One of the two prisoners answered meekly: "We were at the far end of the plant and did not hear the bell. When it became quiet in the plant, we realized we had missed the bell, and so we came back here."

After another day's work at the plant, we were brought by train to a concentration camp in Amsersfoort, Holland.

Chapter Six

Concentration Camp Prisoner

These memoirs were initially printed in the Yad Vashem Studies, Volume 13, in Jerusalem in 1979.

As shocking as conditions were at Amersfoort, Zwolle and Wageningen, it should be remembered that these were labor camps as opposed to extermination camps like Auschwitz-Birkenau, Treblinka, and Sobibor. The overwhelming majority of Jews were sent to extermination camps. Dutch Jews were deported to the transit camp of Westerbork and sent from there to Auschwitz-Birkenau. Extermination camps such as Auschwitz-Birkenau sometimes also served as labor camps where Jews and others who were deemed to be physically fit were enslaved until they weakened. They were then gassed. While prisoners were frequently executed at labor camps such as Amersfoort for not obeying the rules, there were generally no gas chambers there. The overwhelming majority of labor camp prisoners were not Jewish. Jews were only sent to labor camps towards the end of the war when the Germans were on the run and wanted to cover up the existence of the gas chambers.

> I am a religious man, Lutheran, and during the dark days I spent in various prisons, concentration and work camps, I was greatly sustained by my faith.
>
> I recall a beautiful September day in 1944. It was later afternoon and clouds were gracefully sailing along the deep blue sky. However, I could scarcely enjoy the weather or the scenery. I had been standing at attention for hours, along with other prisoners, on the grounds of the concentration camp at Amersfoort. Making us stand in this

fashion was one of the diversions of our German captors. A number of prisoners had already collapsed from the ordeal.

Silently, I addressed myself to God. Combining questions and prayer, I said: "Dear Lord, should I be punished so severely because I tried to save the lives of my friends? What did I do wrong?" I was answered immediately. Before my eyes, a bright white light appeared in the dark blue sky. Suddenly, I felt free of every fear that had previously haunted me. I was overcome by a great sense of security and I knew for certain that I would one day come back to my home, safe and sound.

Amersfoort

The first sight that greeted us at Amersfoort concentration camp was the barbed wire that surrounded it. This barbed wire was three or four rows thick and about three feet of space separated one row from the next. At the front of the camp was an SS guard in a small station.

We saw some wooden shacks and in front of them people were sitting on their suitcases and waiting. Soon we had to join these people and we too waited, filled with apprehension. I utilized the time to familiarize myself with our new surroundings: the wooden shacks, the barbed wire, and the many people behind the barbed wire. I noticed that all these people were running, not walking. They seemed to be in a terrible hurry. Later, I found out that we were in the administration department. In spite of that, the men behind the barbed wire took a chance, ran up to the newcomers and asked for cigarettes or tobacco. Alas, none of us could oblige them. All our tobacco had literally gone up in smoke during the long weeks we had already spent in prisons. I noticed that the men behind the barbed wire looked terribly shabby. Like ours, their heads were shorn. They were clad in the most diverse clothes imaginable. As for fit, the clothes were either too big or too small, and they were torn and dirty. In my mind's eye, I saw myself walking around in a like manner, and I shuddered at the thought.

Finally, we were told to go into one of the shacks, and ordered to hand over all our money and valuables. Since I had no money, I received some dirty looks. The only valuables I had were a watch and my wedding ring. These were taken from me and put aside. Next, girls sitting behind nearby tables, dressed in German uniforms, took down such personal data as name, date and place of birth, residence, etc. Then came the question: "What is the nature of the crime that brought you to Amersfoort?" I answered: "*Judenbegunstigung* (I helped Jewish people)." This won me more dirty looks. Eventually, each of us got a number, which, from then on, would serve as our only identification. My friend Kleiman had the number 7005. Mine was 7006. Later these numbers were sewn on our jackets.

Subsequently, I learned that this was the third series of 30,000, so that my number was really 67,006. In other words, 67,004 people had preceded us at this concentration camp. I have often wondered where some of these people are, and, indeed, how many of them remained alive.

Then we were sent to another shack where we had to undress, put our clothes in a paper bag and hand it in. The bags were marked with our respective numbers and stowed away. After that, we were ordered to go outside, in the nude. For a full hour, we stood naked. Luckily, it was a fine summer day and the sun was shining. What if it had been colder, or raining, even snowing? Why were we kept waiting outside naked for an hour? The answer was clear: It was noon, and our German captors were enjoying their lunch.

Now came the time for our clothing. The man in charge of trousers threw a pair at you. Too long, too wide, too short or too tight. It mattered little. You had to take them and depend on your ingenuity. Next, we got the most diverse jackets. For example, I was given a tunic like the ones worn by Amsterdam streetcar conductors. A third man gave us caps, while the fourth completed our attire by throwing old wooden shoes at us. You had to take them whether they fit or not. I was lucky. Everything I received fit quite well. The same was true for Mr. Kleiman. Even so, we looked at one other dressed in our new garb and the sight was most depressing.

After handing out clothes, one of the men shouted at us: "Have a good look at your things; there may be lice in them." And, indeed, on the other side of the fence, we noticed several people inspecting their shirts and hunting for those creeping and uninvited guests. Luckily, the only time I found lice in my clothes was at the end of my stay at Amersfoort concentration camp.

We were told to form rows of three and were led through the second barbed wire fence. We had to go through very small openings in the fence, and these were heavily guarded. Now we came into an oblong space which was also protected by barbed wire. This was the so-called "Rose Garden," a euphemism for a place that was feared by every prisoner in the Amersfoort concentration camp. For it was in the "Rose Garden" that punishments were meted out by our German captors. We had been brought here because for the moment they did not know what to do with us.

Meanwhile, we had an opportunity to observe life in the camp. Just in front of us was the large, open square where the roll calls, so important in the camp routine, were held. We noticed that anyone passing this square did not walk, but ran, sometimes chased by another prisoner with a wooden club in his hand. These "clubbers," as they were called, collaborated with the Germans, and were detested by the prisoners. At night, when they had to be together with the rest of us, nobody spoke to them. And other than perhaps getting a bit more food or better clothing, they got no preferential treatment from the Gestapo, for these "clubbers" were also despised by the Germans.

We must have stood for at least two hours in the "Rose Garden." We heard the Gestapo shouting commands in German and the prisoners did their best to obey. If they were not quick enough in executing these commands, the prisoners were rewarded with swift strokes of the wooden clubs. This, then, was our first lesson in Amersfoort concentration camp.

Finally, we were taken from the "Rose Garden" to several shacks, which were to be our quarters. Each shack contained two rooms, one large and one small. In the large room there were four long rows of beds, mostly *double- or triple-decker* bunks. Mr. Kleiman and I were placed in the small room which contained eight *triple-decker* bunks. I was given an upper bunk, just beside a small window, facing a double barbed wire fence, which we were told was electrically charged. Through the window I could also see a high watchtower, with machine guns and floodlights.

In each room, big or small, one of the prisoners was in charge of tidiness, etc. He instructed us on how to behave inside the camp, and how to make our beds in the morning. More important than telling us what to do were his instructions about what not to do and whom to avoid. For example, he warned us about a Gestapo man named Atulia. He was a little man, just five feet tall, always walking with a stick under his arm, and a German shepherd dog at his side. This dog was specially trained. When he saw a prisoner walking outside, he immediately attacked him and tried to tear off his trousers. If the prisoner incited this dog in any way, he jumped at the prisoner's throat and bit him. This resulted in many a bloody face. Such a spectacle was very much enjoyed by the Gestapo and they laughed heartily at the fear displayed by the prisoners being attacked.

It was time for our first lunch. This was short and frugal — a few slices of bread and coffee substitute. Supper arrived in big tins and was distributed in metal bowls, out of which we ate. The "meal" consisted of a watery, tasteless something, with a few little pieces of potato floating around in it. Kleiman and I sat together, on a lower bunk bed, the metal bowls on our knees as we spooned up our supper. Kleiman had stomach trouble. He had had two operations and part of his stomach had been removed. I fished out the few pieces of firm potato I found in my bowl and gave them to him. I felt he needed them much more than I did.

I was put to work in the straw braider's shop. The foreman was not in and I was glad about that because he had a very bad reputation for tyrannizing the workers. He was a Dutch SS man who had deserted, been caught, and sent to Amersfoort. Now he was trying to ingratiate himself with the Germans by being especially cruel to the prisoners. His deputy did not ask much and showed me what I had to do.

One day, there was great unrest in the braiders' shop. The foreman ran around like a wild man, shouting at everyone. He criticized our work and our output. Finally, he left the shop. I thought that it would be a good idea if I disappeared for a while. I pretended that I had to go to the washroom, and on my way there, I saw the foreman coming back with one of the most feared "clubbers." When I returned from the washroom, I noticed that nobody spoke a word and that all of the prisoners were working much faster than usual. Therefore I also sped up my tempo. After a while, I looked around and I immediately knew what had happened during my short absence.

That clubber had been brought in and he had done a good job. Two men had bleeding wounds on their heads. One man was rubbing his back, and another man was limping. I thanked God that I had missed this clubber's orgy.

Something had urged me to go out just at the right time, and my going to the washroom had merely been an excuse.

Roll calls took place daily and were a very important part of life in the concentration camp. The first was at six o'clock in the morning and was held outside, in the aforementioned large open square, as were the next two, at noon and early evening. Then, at ten P.M., there was a fourth roll call, in the shacks. As we assembled for the first roll call it was not yet six in the morning, but already the "clubbers" in command were waiting along the rows of prisoners, shouting, swearing, and giving orders. Anyone slow to obey was quickly acquainted with their clubs.

Nor was this the real muster. That was done by the Germans themselves. We often had to wait for hours for them. When the first German command was heard, we knew this was the start of the roll call, and for us prisoners it was dead serious. First, we would hear "*Stillgestanden!*" This meant click your heels together, no matter what you have on your feet, be it wooden shoes or leather. The most important part of this command was to stand at attention. Then came a series of other commands and each had to be executed quickly, with German precision. Then the real muster began. The first man in the front row started counting: in Dutch, "*een,*" the next man said "*twee,*" "*drie,*" etc. A German officer walked around during the counting and woe betide the prisoner who displeased him in any way.

During the roll calls, various announcements were made. Then the Germans went back to their quarters. The prisoners, about thirty-five hundred at the time I was at the concentration camp, were left standing, often at attention, for hours at a time. The longest wait I experienced was two and a quarter hours. It was quite common for prisoners to faint from sheer exhaustion or exposure. Once a man standing next to me lost consciousness. I dragged him to a shack and placed him on the ground next to a wall, in the shade.

Once, a roll call was taken by a "German" who was really a Dutch SS man in German uniform. He was a former bicycle repairman, and he tried to imitate the German shouting and clubbing as much as possible. Suddenly, he heard sirens, and saw a lone Allied Spitfire circling above us. An object came tumbling down, which later turned out to be an empty fuel can. The moment the sirens sounded, the Germans ran to their blockhouses, but we, the prisoners, were not allowed to take shelter. We had to stay where we were. Meanwhile, our quasi-German did not know where to run, so he fled towards the kitchen wall, which was made of brick, and hid behind some dahlia bushes in front of it. We all smiled. Some of us even dared to laugh loudly. It was a funny sight: a member of Hitler's own elite guard, his SS Schutzstaffel — each of whom was considered to be afraid of nothing, not even of the devil himself — creeping like a dog and hiding behind dahlias!

In a little while, the Spitfire disappeared and the air-raid alarm ended. The "heroes" came out of their hiding places and the "fun" began. For them, that is; not for us, the prisoners.

The Germans shouted: "You swine, you had a good laugh, did you? Now we'll really give you something to enjoy. We'll teach you what it means to laugh when you are supposed to be standing at attention!" Then a hail of blows from their sticks and truncheons came down on the heads of the poor prisoners. Those of us who tried to raise our arms to protect ourselves only made matters worse, and the clubs descended upon us with even greater vengeance.

We remembered that episode for a long time. Catching a few blows from a club was nearly a daily occurrence for us prisoners. But that particular sadistic clubbing is one we never forgot.

In retrospect, I see a great chain of events that worked to save me from death and lead me to freedom. Here is just one example:

The concentration camp at Amersfoort was actually a collection center. Prisoners from different points were brought to Amersfoort and from there they were destined to proceed to concentration and extermination camps in Germany. Amersfoort was a very important railway intersection in Holland. On September 17, 1944, at noon, American planes flew over and bombed the main railway station and yards. A transport of prisoners, about eleven hundred men (myself among them) were standing ready to be shipped to Germany that night. But now this was impossible, because of the American bombs. Dutch Kamp Polizei working with the Germans went around with clubs in their hands and mercilessly clubbed the heads of any prisoners who walked slowly or were not quite in line. As a result, the Netherlands Red Cross intervened on humanitarian grounds. These two factors — the American bombing action and the intervention of the Red Cross — succeeded in keeping the prisoners of this special transport in Holland. We were sent north, to the forced labor camp at Zwolle and later to the one at Wageningen.

Zwolle

It was about five o'clock in the morning when we arrived in Zwolle. We were taken to a former movie theater, which was to be our quarters. The seats had been removed from the theater and bales of straw brought in.

More than one thousand men slept on this straw, and there were only three washrooms for all of us. At seven A.M., we lined up for coffee and two slices of bread. Then there was a roll call similar to those taken at Amersfoort concentration camp.

However, in general, life at Zwolle was heaven compared to life at Amersfoort. Our work consisted mostly of digging tank traps outside the city of Zwolle. As we marched to and from work, we were ordered to sing, and all the while we were accompanied by German guards.

Civilians often stood at the side of the road and watched us. At Zwolle, we wore our former civilian clothes, which had been given back to us. Among us were two young prisoners in their twenties, dressed in long Catholic clerical garb. They attracted a great deal of attention. Shortly thereafter, these two young men disappeared. The next day, the chaplain of the church was picked up. He was beaten, brought to our quarters, and put to work. The Germans told him, "The two boys come back, or you keep on working here." The boys came back.

At one time, a few other men and I were put to work assembling bicycles. The Germans had quite a system of obtaining bicycles: a soldier seeing any cyclist simply ordered him off the bicycle and took it away. I recall one day when the haul was more than two dozen. By that stage of the war most of the bicycles had seen better days, and tires had not been available for years. We were told to remove the good parts and assemble them into roadworthy bicycles.

At Zwolle we were deluged with food by the townspeople. They brought us bread, slices of cheese, fruit, and jugs of milk. It was an outpouring of kindness from the Dutch people towards the prisoners. In this way, these goodhearted people gave vent to their pent-up feelings; on the one hand, their anger and hostility towards the occupying German forces, and on the other hand, their wholehearted sympathy and compassion for us, who were held prisoner in this forced labor camp at Zwolle. Nor were our spiritual needs neglected. A Protestant minister and a Catholic priest came in regularly and held services. I still have the little pocket Bible that I received at the Zwolle forced labor camp.

In time, the straw on which we slept became pulverized and the dust swirled around us, causing many sore throats. At night there was much coughing. It was impossible to sleep. Thanks to the Netherlands Red Cross, this situation was soon rectified. They took out the old straw, thoroughly cleaned and disinfected the floor, and then brought in new bales.

And when they saw that we had nothing with which to cover ourselves, they furnished us with cotton covers, which were quite warm.

Most of the forced laborers at Zwolle were young men who had been picked up in manhunts. In the fall of 1944, the Germans organized manhunts in all of the big cities of Holland. German soldiers, called Grüne Polizei (Green Police) because of their green uniforms, picked up all the young men they could find. The average age of the victims was about twenty-five.

The Germans needed slave labor for their war industry in Germany, so that they could put their own men into military service. This was forbidden by international law, but the Germans cared little about such a "technicality."

Many of the boys who were thus picked up finally landed in the forced labor camp at Zwolle. They had been caught during the manhunts in the big cities of Rotterdam and Amsterdam. Some of them had even been chased over the roofs of houses and buildings by the Germans, until they were finally caught by the Grüne Polizei.

The prisoners from the concentration camp at Amersfoort were either political prisoners, in the sense that they had disobeyed German orders by listening to the radio or distributing leaflets for the Dutch Underground movement, etc., or people like myself, whose crime had been to help Jews. When we arrived at Zwolle, we were eventually mixed with the Zwolle workers and in time nobody knew why any particular prisoner was in that forced labor camp. This could only be beneficial to prisoners like myself, who came from the Amersfoort concentration camp. The Germans tended to regard all "Amersfoorters" as criminals, and now they did not know who was who.

During the eight months I spent in prisons, forced labor and concentration camps, I learned to listen carefully, and speak little. You never knew the political views of your fellow prisoners.

Occasionally the Germans threw in "prisoners" who were actually there for the sole purpose of finding out our political opinions. This was a trick used by the Germans to find out what we thought of them. I once spotted such a decoy in my own cell. A few days after being brought to my cell, he was taken out for a so-called interrogation, and I never saw him again. He had questioned me at length about the war and politics. Luckily, I suspected him right from the start and my answers were noncommittal.

In time, I got to know most of the boys at Zwolle and indeed, became good friends with a number of them. I often had confidential talks with them, mostly about politics, especially since our views were similar. I made friends with one man who had been an active member of the Dutch resistance movement and had many useful contacts outside. This man, whom I shall call Mr. X, proved very useful to me later on.

Wageningen

The work at Zwolle finished rather abruptly and we were sent to Wageningen, another forced labor camp in Holland. There, I was particularly lucky. Soon after I arrived at Wageningen, the Lagerführer (Camp Commander) called me into his office and said: "I need a trustworthy person who speaks fluent German and Dutch and who would deliver daily messages to the headquarters of the O.T. (Organization Todt, a group that worked for the army, digging trenches and tank traps)."

He added: "I have chosen you for the job. The headquarters are at Ede, about four miles from here."

So, a few days later, I became the messenger boy for the German commander. I also worked in the office. I was given a bicycle, identification papers and a green ribbon to be put around my left arm. The ribbon carried a written authorization, stating that I was allowed to pass through the villages of Wageningen and Bennekom. These villages had now been evacuated for three months. The reason: in September 1944, British paratroopers landed there for the raid on Arnhem, a Dutch city located along the Rhine River. The Allies were enthusiastically received and helped by the people of Wageningen and Bennekom, and for this, the Germans meted out swift punishment. The people were forced to vacate their homes and the two villages became ghost towns.

The Lagerführer asked me to introduce myself to all the prisoners. He also gave me cigarettes and asked me to distribute them among the boys. After finishing this, my first official task, I was subjected to a tongue-lashing by some of my acquaintances from our previous work camp at Zwolle, where we had often had confidential talks. They asked me, "How come you are now working with the Germans, and in Zwolle you were so much against them?"

I answered: "I am still the same man you knew at Zwolle. The only difference is that here I shall have an opportunity to help the boys wherever I can. If there is something I can do for you, let me know."

There was a lot of paperwork at Wageningen and I was taking over more and more responsibilities; this way I had more latitude. Also, the Lagerführer was a former gardener, and he was quite content to leave the running of the office to me. I needed extra help and I took advantage of this fact. I stretched the office work as much as I could and every day I asked for extra people to help me. By keeping many of the boys in the office, I cheated the Germans out of forced labor in the fields. This particular job for which the Lagerführer had chosen me afforded me a rare opportunity. Because of my work, I was able to help our people in many ways. At the same time I did as much as I could to cheat and outwit the Germans. I was, therefore, determined to hold on to my job.

I now turned my attention to the matter of outstanding wages that were owed us from the forced labor camp at Zwolle. Because we had been transported very abruptly from Zwolle to Wageningen, the Germans still owed us one and a half weeks' wages. As workers in a forced labor camp, we were paid five Dutch guilders a day (seven and a half guilders for working on Sunday). I put in a request for the prisoners' outstanding wages and they all received their back pay in full.

Flushed with success, I grew bolder and asked for something even more important than back wages. I asked for our identification papers, which had been taken from us when he had arrived at Zwolle, more than three months before. To my great surprise and relief, I received them. One day, when I was picking up the daily mail from the post office at Ede, I was handed a package from Zwolle. It contained all the identification papers, mine included! The Germans at Wageningen knew nothing about all this, so I had to play it cool. I waited for two weeks, holding on to these precious papers. Then I started handing them out to the boys I knew very well and I asked them not to tell anybody about it.

Eventually, I returned all the remaining identification papers to their legitimate owners.

Then the very thing which I had expected, and was afraid of, happened. The boys, once they were again in possession of their papers — the ones called *persoonsebewijs* (personal identification), without which nobody could get ration cards for food, etc. — did not wait long and started to disappear. Within a short while it became noticeable during the morning roll calls that the workers were far fewer in number. The German foreman asked me, "Have you any idea why the number of workers has decreased so markedly?" I said, "I haven't the faintest idea." Obviously they knew nothing about the identification papers that I had received from Zwolle and had distributed.

The next Sunday, however, our labor force was quickly replenished. The Germans applied one of their usual methods to catching men for forced labor. On Sundays, they stood at church doors and waited until the services were over. When the people started coming out, the Germans simply picked the men they needed. So our roll call was not only complete, it grew longer.

Reports had to be sent daily to the headquarters in Ede, giving the exact number of people in our labor camp. Based on these figures, we were sent bread and other food. The "other food" usually consisted of a carload of dry bones for making soup. Right from the outset, I slowly started to report higher numbers of people than were actually present in order to obtain more food. Luckily, the Lagerführer signed all these reports without verifying them. Eventually, I was listing two hundred more men on the reports than were actually present. I kept the numbers at this level and did not exaggerate further.

Part of my work was sending out reports on the various groups that went out to work. In this connection, I questioned the men as to the number of workers in their group, where they worked and what kind of work they did. Needless to say, whatever information seemed important to me went to my middleman, Mr. X, whom I had met at Zwolle and who, like myself, was now at Wageningen. Mr. X always made sure that the vital information I gave him reached the underground resistance movement.

When we first arrived at Wageningen, we stayed in the Plantenziektenkundige Dienst (the Research Center for Plant Diseases). In order to provide sleeping quarters for the prisoners, we were ordered to empty the rooms of all superfluous items. In the corridors there were big showcases with sliding doors. Inside these showcases were books and collections of moths, fungi, and various things that cause diseases in plants. The Germans gave orders to "throw all that stuff out the window and have it burned."

I just could not bear to see the destruction of all these valuable scientific collections, so I said to the boys who were in charge of this operation: "Take all these collections and put them in the shacks at the back of the building." Some of the boys objected. They said, "The Germans ordered us to burn the stuff." I said: "Never mind. The Germans don't care what happens to these collections. All they care about is more space for sleeping quarters. So do as I say. Place the collections in the shacks and if you have any trouble with the Germans, tell me and I shall talk to them!" The boys gave in and the greater part of these scientific collections was stowed away in the shacks behind the building. Years later, I met an official of this government institute and asked him about them. I was glad to learn that the collections had been found in good condition and placed back where they belonged.

The village of Wageningen is situated in the main district where tobacco is grown. At that time (in the first months of 1945) there were no cigarettes or cigars available. The only means of obtaining them was on the black market or under the counter. Consequently, many inhabitants of Wageningen grew tobacco in their backyards for the purpose of rolling their own cigarettes. The tobacco crops had already been taken in when the Germans had evacuated Wageningen some three months before. The former inhabitants of the village had left behind their homes and belongings, including their tobacco crops.

When we arrived, the abandoned tobacco crops were still hanging in the basements drying. The Lagerführer sent out an "organizing group" made up of one German and four or five Dutch prisoners, to search the evacuated homes of Wageningen for food and other articles. "Organizing group" was the euphemism used by the Germans when they sent out small groups to search houses that had been evacuated. When our organizing group returned to the camp, they brought back some of the tobacco leaves they had found in the basements. I noticed that the boys were rolling their own cigarettes and I asked them to keep bringing back tobacco from their home searches. One Dutch prisoner saw what was going on and he came to me and told me that he was a cigar maker by profession. So I decided to keep him busy making hand-rolled cigars. I set aside a table in the corner of the office for this man, and he was occupied all day making fine Dutch cigars. He was only too happy to be doing this rather than digging trenches in the deep snow for the benefit of the Germans.

The Lagerführer rarely came into the office. However, one day he came in to ask me something. He saw me puffing away on a cigar and in the corner of the office, he spotted the cigar maker busily engaged in rolling them. "What's going on here? Are you running an office or a small cigar factory?"

I said, "The organizing group brought back some fine tobacco, and since this man is a professional cigar maker, I decided to utilize his skill."

Much to my surprise, the Lagerführer's expression changed from one of disapproval to one of approval, and he said, "Let him make some cigars for us, too!" (Meaning himself and his friends.)

Looking back, I like to recall the many occasions on which I had a chance to outwit the Germans and help the Allies. One such occasion was the second day after our arrival at Wageningen. I had been assigned by the Lagerführer to work in the office, but my duties were not to begin until the following Monday. After the roll call on that particular Saturday morning, we were asked, "Are there any electricians among you?" About twenty men stepped forward, I among them. (I am quite a good amateur electrician. During my service in the navy, in the First World War, I had had a good deal to do with electrical work.) A German soldier with a rifle under his arm said to us, "Follow me!"

He warned us not to leave the small trail and not to use the road with its tracks of horse carts, because, he said, there were mines along it. After a while, we passed a place in the bush where we heard the unmistakable loud firing of cannons, at regular intervals.

On the south bank of the Rhine, there was a wide stretch of no-man's-land that was held under fire by the Germans. German patrols crossed the Rhine, and sometimes British patrols came over for reconnaissance purposes.

Finally, we arrived at a small castle situated in the bush. For some reason, the connection with the main electrical cable was interrupted and this had to be repaired. A short distance away there was a transformer station. I was told to go inside the castle, into a very large room which I noticed had been transformed into an office. There was a telephone on every desk.

My specific task was to make connections from the main outlet in the entrance hall of the castle to the desk lamps in that room. I also had to repair the connection from the main hall to the chandelier in the center of the ceiling. There was no ladder available, so I took off my shoes and in my stocking feet I climbed onto a chair placed on the table in order to reach the ceiling. From my vantage point in the center of the room, I could see all the desks with the telephones. What was more, I could hear the many incoming and outgoing calls. It became clear to me that this was an important command post. I therefore kept my ears open and dawdled over my work as long as I possibly could. I wanted to hear as much as possible, but I had to be careful not to arouse suspicion.

Meanwhile, I mentally stored away whatever information might be of importance to the Allies. I realized the significance of this command post and of the entrance to the bush. I resolved that they must be destroyed. I returned to Mr. X (of the Dutch Underground) and lost no time in telling him about the cannons in the bush, the command post, and what I had heard. All this information quickly found its way into the right channels.

A few days later, I was pleased to learn that the big guns in the bush had been silenced by Allied planes, and the cable connections to the castle were again interrupted.

About the middle of March 1945, we heard rumors that the work in Wageningen was finished and that we were to move further west. We were glad about that because the "west" meant populated districts. We would see more people, perhaps even our relatives and friends, and we would have a better idea of what was actually happening.

I had learned in this war that every rumor bears a grain of truth. Within a few days this was verified for me. Every man was ordered to appear the next morning, at seven o'clock, in front of the building, and to have with him all the essential possessions he could carry. The move was on. I took a bicycle with me and I advised a friend of mine to do the same. I said, "You never know when we might need these bicycles." We both kept to the end of the line, for it was our definite intention to escape if possible.

Escape

The Dutch railway men were on strike at the time, by order of the Dutch Government in Exile in London. Consequently, we prisoners, a column of about six hundred men, had to walk through the city of Arnhem along the north bank of the Rhine. We had reached the last Dutch village, Zevenaar, and within a short while we were to cross over into Germany. This was a grim prospect indeed.

But once again, I was lucky.

Our column was attacked by British Spitfires. In the confusion that followed, my friend and I escaped. Holding on to our bicycles, we ran between two houses and hid in an outbuilding until we felt it was safe to continue our journey, which we hoped would bring us safely home.

Our travels were fraught with danger, and we might never have reached our destination were it not for the friendly farmers and villagers who helped us along the way. They were known as "the good people." They would shelter us for a day or two, then send us along to other "good people," who looked after our needs and safety.

There were so many to whom we were indebted. There was the farmer who provided us with inconspicuous clothing. Another sheltered us in his barn. Later, his wife gave us a good breakfast. She also filled my thermos bottle with something piping hot that tasted like tea and provided me and my friend with several eggs for our continuing journey. Then there was the lady who warned us that the road we were traveling on was dangerous because of too much German traffic. She advised us to go to the village of Giesbook in the opposite direction, and we took her advice.

I also remember the young boy who directed us to a large brick kiln near the Rhine River. There, bricks were made from the clay on the river bank. We hid in this kiln until nightfall before resuming our journey, this time across the river.

As we waited in the brick kiln, along with a number of other people who were escaping, many hours stretched before us, so I opened the bundle that contained my few possessions and started to darn all my socks and mend my clothes. All the while I kept thinking that I would soon be back in my home town of Hilversum and after so many months in prisons, concentration and forced labor camps, I would see my wife and friends again.

My faith was justified and before long I was ringing the doorbell of my house. However, nobody opened the door. Soon my neighbor's wife appeared and told me that my wife was with them because she was not well and could not be left at home alone. The next day I started to prepare a hiding place in my house for myself and my wife. Should the Germans come to take me back, I was determined that they would not find me.

However, my preparations proved unnecessary, because four weeks later, on May 6, 1945, the Germans surrendered, at Wageningen, to Canadian General Foulkes and HRH Prince Bernhard of the Netherlands. The German general who surrendered [*as Hitler had committed suicide ten days before — ed.*] was Johannes Blaskowitz.

Chapter Seven

Liberation and Revelation

Holland was liberated on May 6, 1945, shortly before the end of the war, by Allied forces that contained a large Canadian contingent. To this day, the Dutch people fondly remember the brave role played by Canadian troops in fighting the last remnants of German Nazi tyranny.

On October 1, 1946, the International Military Tribunal in Nuremberg sentenced Artur Seyss-Inquart to death by hanging. Other German war criminals — Goering, Ribbentrop, Keitel, Kaltenbrunner, Streicher, and others — received similar sentences. Goering committed suicide by taking poison on October 15. On October 16, 1946, the sentences for the other Nazi kingpins were carried out. By three A.M., they were executed.

For Victor Kugler personally, the end of the war ended the period in which he had felt he could not talk to his wife about a large portion of his life: about sheltering the Franks and the terrible consequences of doing so. Not that their separation during his imprisonment had been complete. On Evelyn Wolfe's tape, he said his wife had been allowed to visit him every two weeks.

On the surface, the end of the war seemed to mean it was now possible to resume normal life in Holland.

But the evil perpetrated by Seyss-Inquart had been accomplished. Holland's Jewish population was only a quarter of what it had been before the war. Immediately after liberation, Victor Kugler set out to learn what had happened to the Dutch Jews he had sheltered for twenty-five months.

The Shattered Remnant

Of the eight people sheltered in the Secret Annex, only Otto Frank survived.

He was at Auschwitz when it was liberated by the Red Army on January 29, 1945. He returned to Amsterdam in June 1945 and reestablished contact with Henk and Miep Gies and Victor Kugler. Victor Kugler's memoirs as told to Eda Shapiro pick up the story:

> Only in July 1945 did Otto learn about Anne's grim fate. From the remnants left by the Holocaust, we found out how Anne Frank's last months on earth had been spent. She had been in concentration camps, moving from Westerbork in Holland, to Auschwitz in Poland, to Bergen-Belsen in Hanover, Germany. Like the survivors, she was shipped by cattle train to the inferno of Auschwitz. She suffered hunger, degradation and pain. And she witnessed unspeakable horrors.
>
> But unlike the survivors, she was not destined to hold out until *liberation*. Instead, her short life ended in Bergen-Belsen in March 1945, two months beforehand, just like her sister Margot's. On arrival at Auschwitz, like all the prisoners, Margot and Anne had their hair cut off, to be used for packing pipe joints and making machine belts. A survivor recalls standing with the sisters as they watched a group of naked Gypsy girls (the Gypsies were another hate of Hitler's [*even though if any ethnic group can claim to be of pure Indo-Aryan stock it is them — ed.*]), being herded to the gas chambers. There was also a group of small children huddled around the doors, waiting, because it was not yet their turn to be executed.
>
> Anne could only exclaim, "Look, look at their eyes!"
>
> By now, the Russians were advancing rapidly towards Auschwitz. The crematoriums, already working at full blast, could not dispose of the inmates fast enough. Margot and Anne were among those shipped on to Bergen-Belsen.
>
> Mr. Otto Frank, who was in the hospital barracks, was still alive when the Russians arrived. He was taken to Odessa and put on a French ship for Marseille. From there he made his way back to Amsterdam — the only one to survive.

The following is a combination of Evelyn Wolfe's taped interview and Eda Shapiro's written account:

When Mr. Frank returned to Amsterdam, a survivor from Bergen-Belsen who had befriended Anne and Margot Frank visited him as soon as she knew of his whereabouts. Mr. Frank learned from her what had happened to his daughters.

Margot had contracted typhus from the terrible living conditions, and died. For Anne, this was the final blow. She announced, "I will not live any longer." Within a week she was dead of the same disease.

The Diary Survives

The following paragraphs are quoted from Richard Amdur's biography of Anne Frank. These events took place immediately after Victor Kugler and Johannes Kleiman were arrested and taken away from the Secret Annex on August 4, 1944:

> Silberbauer, joining the group, ordered Otto Frank to reveal where the Jews kept their valuables. Then he picked up Mr. Frank's briefcase and scattered its contents — Anne's diaries and papers — onto the floor. In their place he put the Jews' jewelry and money. Anne and the others were then allowed to pack some clothing and toiletries. A vehicle had been summoned and was on its way.
>
> A little while later, Silberbauer addressed Miep downstairs. "Aren't you ashamed that you are helping Jewish garbage?" he said with a snarl. "You have betrayed your country. You deserve the worst."
>
> But when the transport arrived and the eight Jews, Kraler (Kugler) and Koophuis (Kleiman) were taken away to Gestapo headquarters, Miep was not among them. She had recognized Silberbauer's accent as that of someone from Vienna. She, too, was Viennese, and she told him as much. Silberbauer seemed to calm down. Apparently, this was enough to win Miep a reprieve. But Silberbauer parted with a warning: "As a personal favor, I'm going to let you stay here, but if you run away, we'll take your husband. I know he's involved."
>
> With the Nazis gone, Miep and Elli went with a workman, who

had the keys, up to the Secret Annex. They had to hurry. The Nazis might return at any moment. The place had been ransacked in the search for more valuables. On the floor of what had been the Franks' bedroom, Miep noticed the papers, notebooks and diaries Anne had filled with her writings. Quickly, Miep and Elli gathered everything they could and put them in Miep's desk down at the office. A few days later, Miep went upstairs again to retrieve still more of Anne's papers. "I'll keep everything safe for Anne until she comes back," she told herself and put them in a drawer.

A few days later, a truck sent by the Nazi authorities came back to the Secret Annex and carted off all of the Jews' remaining belongings.

Miep and Henk Gies kept the diary throughout the war. When Otto returned, they gave it back to him. Otto Frank and Victor Kugler regained and retained contact. In the following account, from Evelyn Wolfe's taped interview, Victor Kugler describes how Otto Frank initially had the *Diary of Anne Frank* published:

> After the war, over nine hundred diaries were found throughout Amsterdam written by Jews in hiding.
>
> Soon after Miep Gies gave the diary of Anne's writings to Otto Frank, he gave it to a friend to read, and that friend gave it to another friend who was a professor of literature at the university and also a radio speaker. The professor read it and told Mr. Frank that he was "very moved. This must be published."
>
> The first publisher to whom the diary was submitted refused it. The third or fourth accepted it.

In 1947, Contact Publishers of Amsterdam published *Het Achterhuis: Dagboekbrieven van 12 Juni 1942 — 1 Augustus 1944* (The Secret Annex: diary notes from 12 June 1942 — 1 August 1944) which became a best seller and in 1952 was translated into English as *Anne Frank: The Diary of a Young Girl*. As of this writing, over thirty million copies have been sold worldwide, according to the Anne Frank Center, and the stage and film adaptations have also enjoyed broad success — we will later discuss how these related to Victor Kugler. Suffice it to say that the world at large did not know exactly what had happened to the residents of the Secret Annex until 1957, ten years after the initial Dutch publication of the diary.

In the spring of 1957, *Time* magazine, in the "Historical Notes" column in its foreign news section, published a half-page account of the deportations of Anne and Margot to Auschwitz and their deaths in Bergen-Belsen. Then, in its August 19, 1957 edition, *Time*'s sister publication, *Life*, a weekly news picture magazine, which was then the world's single most influential periodical, ran a major cover feature entitled "What Happened to Anne Frank after the Diary." The black and white cover featured the famous page from Anne's diary, written in Dutch, along with a photo of her. The text read:

> This is a photo as I would wish myself to look all the time. Then I would maybe have a chance to come to Hollywood.

Reticence

Until then, the full horrific story of the Holocaust had been kept "under cover." True, Lord Russell of Liverpool had written a book entitled *The Scourge of the Swastika* right after the war. It contained some graphic, gruesome accounts of the camps liberated by the British, Canadian and American forces. Orthodox Jewish groups had supplied similar vivid accounts of the German atrocities, but mainstream publishers shied away from offering any of these accounts any form of mass distribution.

There were several reasons for this initial reticence about exposing the greatest crime ever committed in world history. Even though Nazi Germany was now the defeated enemy, a residue of anti-Semitism remained throughout establishment Western society in the immediate postwar years. There was also a feeling of guilt in leading Allied political and military circles for having failed to admit the masses of Jewish refugees into the various Allied countries just before the war. Hiding the facts of the Holocaust was a means of downplaying this guilt. It was necessary for a new generation, which had not been in control in the 1930s and which had relatively clean hands in this respect, to assume control of leading media circles before things could change.

Jewish groups were also ambiguous about exposing the Holocaust. There were fears of exacerbating anti-Semitism and jeopardizing what for many

Jews were newly acquired positions of unprecedented security in postwar society. There was also a feeling that to reveal the Holocaust was tantamount to exposing Jewish vulnerability and powerlessness at a period during which it was necessary to present an image of Jewish strength at all costs. As noted above, Orthodox Jews had exposed the Holocaust even before the death camps were terminated by the Allies. But they were shunned by more assimilated Jewish organizations as being "old-fashioned" and "not American enough," so their views were discredited in "more sophisticated" circles.

In addition, extreme left-wing cultural and political groups, which were much more influential in Jewish society than they are today, tended to adopt the Soviet line that all European peoples were victims of Hitler, not just the Jews. Emphasizing the more historically accurate, uniquely Jewish dimension of the Holocaust, and stating that, while Hitler meant other non-Germanic peoples for enslavement, he had singled out the Jews and Gypsies for extermination, would have been perceived as an attempt to undermine the bonds of the international proletarian solidarity that was the Soviet and Jewish leftist ideal. In other words, the left would have seen it as a sign of Jewish parochial betrayal of other nations. (Needless to say, despite their catering to this line, Stalin executed Soviet Jewish writers anyway, including members of his own Jewish Anti-Fascist Committee, which parroted it most enthusiastically.)

The one notable exception to this rule on the Jewish left was Hashomer Hatzair, whose members had been among the leaders of the Warsaw ghetto uprising. In North America, however, Hashomer Hatzair was considered to be a student fringe group which, ironically, for all its forthright Zionist nationalism, was shunned by many of those same left-leaning Jewish intellectuals who were themselves victimized during the McCarthy anti-communist witch-hunt.

This universalist as opposed to specifically Jewish outlook on the Holocaust even pervaded the best-known dramatization of the diary, that of Frances Goodrich and Albert Hackett. More about the play and Victor Kugler's reaction to it will be detailed in the next chapter.

In this climate of universalism, exposure of the Holocaust as a specifically Jewish tragedy had to wait until an establishment American publication, *Life*, whose right-wing editor-publisher Henry Luce valued and respected the unsurpassed talent and industriousness of his Jewish writers and photographers, decided to deal with this hitherto taboo topic. The release of the story in the summer of 1957 was followed by a flurry of both fictional (*Exodus, The Wall, Mila 18*) and historical studies that dealt with the central, specifically Jewish aspects of the Holocaust.

Hence it was only after 1957, in what was then the colonial cultural backwater of Toronto — for Toronto did not hit its stride as any sort of internationally reputed cultural center until the early 1960s, when it nurtured some popular folk singers — only then did a quietly modest but methodically successful immigrant named Victor Kugler feel confident enough to expose his own story of heroism during the Holocaust.

Chapter Eight

Relocation to Canada

The postwar years, marked by anti-imperial sentiment in the wake of the defeat of the German Nazi empire, were not good years economically. They were particularly difficult for Britain and the Netherlands, who almost immediately lost major overseas colonies. The vast Dutch colony of Indonesia, which had been Holland's major economic agricultural foundation before the war, successfully revolted and won its independence under the leadership of Sukarno, who was to become its first president.

According to Victor Kugler's initial German biographer, Ernst Schnabel, as soon as the war was over, in May 1945, Otto Frank reassumed his controlling partnership of the Opekta spice business, together with Victor Kugler. But business was directly affected by this faraway revolution. Indonesia nationalized its spice industry and severed all ties with its former colonizer. Victor Kugler related to Eda Shapiro:

> Although I was now a free man, life in general was not too bright for me. My wife, who had been ailing, died just three weeks before our twenty-fifth anniversary.
>
> Things were not going well for me in Holland. Spice imports, which formed the bulk of my business, had come to a standstill. Spices (which before came from Indonesia) were simply not available. From year to year, it became harder for me to make a living in my own country. I thought I had better look to other horizons. By that time, I was married to my second wife, Lucy.

Lucy van Langen was born in Amsterdam in 1927. She was twenty-seven years younger than Victor, the eldest of three children, all of whom emigrated to Toronto. Her youngest sibling, Rita, at the time of writing, lives in Streetsville, Ontario. Streetsville, a quiet village twenty-five miles west of Toronto, was incorporated into the thriving suburb of Mississauga during the mid-1970s. According to Rita, who married a Dutch carpenter named Anton Visser before emigrating, "Lucy worked for Opekta, and met Victor there."

Victor and Lucy Kugler were married in 1953. The Opekta business was sold in 1955. At that time, Otto Frank retired. Victor said:

> My wife's brother (Simon, also a carpenter) had moved to Canada, and in 1955, we came to Toronto. Here, I worked for an insurance company and did quite well.

Toronto in the mid-1950s was a rapidly growing city with a solid base of heavy industry. Many European immigrants came here for this reason. They settled in large residential areas in the city's west end, in neighborhoods characterized by endless streets lined with two-story Victorian red-brick semi-detached houses, which, if sometimes crowded, were clean, solidly built and close to the many burgeoning factories. This bucolic residential situation reached its peak, in terms of affordability, from the 1950s to the late 1970s, when Victor Kugler lived in Toronto. It can be argued that this was a golden era for Toronto. Victor and Lucy Kugler settled in Weston, twelve miles northwest of downtown, which was, and largely remains, a mix of industry and quiet, old, tree-lined residential streets.

The Play

Victor Kugler, in his modest fashion, did not go out of his way to publicize his heroism during the war, even when the diary was first published. But soon after he arrived in Toronto, after he had established himself financially, he befriended Leon and Zena Kossar, an East European couple. who later went on to establish North America's oldest urban multicultural festival, Metro Caravan. Countless cities have emulated it. The Kossars did much to open Toronto society to the multiethnic wealth of culture contained within it, and this atmosphere encouraged the shy Victor Kugler to come forward. The friendship that they had with Victor Kugler was a key catalyst in his emergence in Toronto.

Zena Kossar wrote a column for the *Toronto Telegram*, which, under its then-owner, John Bassett Sr., was a populist evening newspaper, one of the most staunchly pro-Jewish and pro-Israel dailies on the continent. Victor Kugler himself told Eda Shapiro what happened as a result of his friendship with the Kossars:

> Shortly after I arrived in Toronto, Canada, in 1956, I received a call from Mr. Leon Kossar of the *Toronto Telegram*. He said: "Mr. Kugler, you probably know that [the play version of] *The Diary of Anne Frank* is being presented. Would you and your wife care to join me and Mrs. Kossar at the performance?"
>
> My feelings were extremely mixed. I had seen the stage play before and recalled how moved I was. An inner voice kept saying to me: "Don't go. Refuse this invitation." At the same time, a "magnet" kept pulling me towards the theater. The magnet won, and Lucy and I found ourselves sitting in Toronto's Royal Alexandra Theatre, alongside Mr. and Mrs. Kossar, in June 1958.
>
> The house lights dimmed. The curtain rose, and on stage I saw a replica of the Secret Annex. I watched actors portraying my friends, now all dead except for Mr. Frank. An actor was even portraying me. I just could not reconcile the make-believe I was seeing on the stage with the stark reality I had witnessed daily. I was sorely tempted to leave the theater. Somehow, I managed to sit through that performance.
>
> The play starred Abigail Kellog as Anne; Francis Lederer played her father, Otto Frank, and Otto Hullett portrayed me, Mr. Kraler. After the performance, we were invited to meet the cast. Mr. Hulett told me: "In all my years as an actor I have never been as nervous as tonight. The knowledge that I was playing a man who was watching me portray him simply terrified me."
>
> Little did Mr. Hulett know how unnerving that evening had been for me, or fathom my pain watching.
>
> As I left the Royal Alexandra Theatre I resolved "never again" to go see any performance of *The Diary of Anne Frank.*

Victor Kugler's reaction is highly significant in the wake of the controversy that surrounded the stage version he saw at Toronto's most famous legitimate theater.

The initial stage adaptation of the diary was written by the staunchly Zionist American Jewish author and playwright Meyer Levin, who was already well established because of his novel about the old Jewish West Side of Chicago, *The Old Bunch*. Despite his credentials, Levin's initial stage adaptation was rejected by assimilationist Broadway producers, Jewish and non-Jewish, whose underlying motives were as I detailed in the previous chapter of this book. They felt that Levin's version, which was true to the diary, was too parochially Jewish, so they had it readapted by the screenwriting couple Frances Goodrich and Albert Hackett. It was more universalist in outlook and left in only a few superficial Jewish references. Otto Frank, understandably eager to spread Anne's message to the world, decided to go along with the Goodrich-Hackett version. Whether his decision was right or wrong in principle vis-à-vis Meyer Levin, I leave to the reader to decide, but in any case, his motives were understandable.

Meyer Levin believed Goodrich and Hackett had plagiarized his version, and launched an unsuccessful lawsuit. Meanwhile, the Goodrich-Hackett version, which Victor Kugler saw in Toronto, was produced on Broadway and became a huge stage and screen hit around the world. When Meyer Levin attempted to stage his original version in Tel Aviv in the mid-1960s, the producers of the Goodrich-Hackett version countersued him. Tragically, Meyer Levin and Otto Frank became adversaries as a result of this long, messy legal case. Meyer Levin may have lost legally, but history ultimately vindicated him, albeit posthumously. Later accounts of the diary and of the life of Anne Frank emphasize the specifically Jewish nature of her tragedy, the way Meyer Levin would have preferred. But Levin's version was not possible in the literary climate of the 1950s, 1960s, or even early 1970s, given the residue of anti-Semitism in both right-wing and left-wing academic-intellectual and media circles. Victor Kugler's negative gut reaction to the Goodrich-Hackett version is, in hindsight, more understandable today than it could have been then.

A version of the Goodrich-Hackett play was revived on Broadway in 1999, revised by Wendy Kesselring to present a somewhat more specifically Jewish context. The young Israeli-born actress Natalie Portman — who later went on to play a leading role in the three blockbuster hit *Star Wars* prequels, and in the early third millennium was perhaps the only Jewish Hollywood actress to defend Israel against campus hostility — played the role of Anne, to rave reviews. The Kesselring version was subsequently produced at Canada's Stratford Festival in 2000, when it starred the late Canadian-Jewish actor Al Waxman (best known for his role in the early 1980s TV series *Cagney and Lacey*) as Otto Frank.

Interestingly enough, Victor Kugler's gut reaction to the symphonic-operatic performance of the musical work *From the Diary of Anne Frank* by the Czech-born Jewish composer Oskar Morawetz, which was premiered in Toronto in 1970, and which emphasized the specifically Jewish nature of her tragedy both musically and thematically, was completely positive.

But there was one redeeming aspect of Victor Kugler's attending the Royal Alexandra performance in 1958.

Sitting on the other side of him was a lady who commented on how moving the story of Anne Frank was.

Victor Kugler said, "I am the man who hid Anne Frank."

She was stunned.

This lady, who was later to play a major role in the life of Victor and Lucy Kugler, was Evelyn Wolfe.

Weston is far from Toronto's Jewish neighborhoods. The initial area of Jewish settlement, Spadina-Kensington, was immediately west of downtown but by the time the Kuglers arrived, most of the city's 100,000-strong Jewish population had moved out of the inner city, directly north into Forest Hill and Cedarvale, and further north along Bathurst Street, one of Toronto's major north-south thoroughfares. Evelyn Wolfe was among those who made this migration. By the mid-1950s she was married and had moved into a house on Robinwood Avenue. It is a quiet, leafy little lane just a mile north of downtown. But it has the distinct atmosphere of fashionable suburbs like Scarsdale, New York, or Chicago's North Shore, which are much further away from their respective downtowns.

The Jewish population of Toronto had established itself as a defiant and strong group, beginning with the riots on August 16, 1933, at Christie Pits, when Nazi sympathizers had unfurled a swastika flag after a baseball game and been shown in no uncertain terms by the Jews in attendance that the Jews of Toronto were not to be tampered with.

This defiantly proud Toronto Jewish community, which was just hitting its stride in the mid-1960s, was the one with which Victor Kugler eventually came into contact. And it was this community that inevitably encouraged a very shy Victor Kugler to reveal his remarkable, defiant life story.

Retirement

The 1960s came and went. Toronto flourished culturally for the first time. This coming-of-age was fuelled by American refugees from the Vietnam War, a sense of Canadian national pride upon its centenary year, an economic boom emanating from the newly signed Canada-US Auto Pact, and a recognition of the city's own urban virtues in having avoided the deterioration of its nearby American counterparts. The city became an exciting but relaxed place to be. Victor Kugler, in his final working years, spoke at various Jewish institutions and met Eda Shapiro through her son Mark. And then, during this good period in Toronto's history, Victor Kugler retired. He told Eda Shapiro:

> Now at age seventy, I had to bow to a company regulation, and reluctantly, I had to leave the business world and retire in 1971. I certainly don't feel seventy. In fact, I never think of age. Instead, I think of the travels my wife and I can now plan. I think of the many books I never had time to read, and which at last I can enjoy. I tend to our house and garden in Weston. Whenever I can, I snatch a few hours a day to work in my darkroom, enjoying my hobby of photography. All in all, it's a good life.

Victor Kugler's sister-in-law, Rita Visser, who was raising a family nearby in Weston, shares the following fond memories of Victor Kugler just before and after his retirement:

> Victor was always nice and talkative. When Lucy had people over, he would join in the conversation. He was friendly to everyone.
>
> Victor liked classical music, and he loved to walk. He was good at languages. He spoke good English, and he had picked up Dutch and knew French. He went to night school and learned Spanish quite well, since he already knew Latin.
>
> Nothing was too much trouble for Victor. He was always ready to help me out, especially when I was pregnant. Victor was very good to

my mother, who came to Canada from Holland in December 1955. She lived with the Kuglers in Toronto. She had asthma, and she died in 1980.

Victor often drove us places. He was strict with my children. He would not let them talk in the car. But my children loved him just the same.

Victor Kugler told Eda Shapiro about his relationship to his past, when he sheltered the Franks, the van Pelses, and Dr. Pfeffer:

> There are many things to remind me of the old days: an item in a newspaper or magazine; a film or new book; the two postcards Anne sent me before the family went into hiding, which I treasure so much. They have her fingerprints on them, with mine added. But most of all, it is letters that link my old life with the new one in Canada. For example, I correspond regularly with Otto Frank. He is now eighty-one years old and lives with his second wife, Fritzie, in Amsterdam. Only last year, my wife and I paid them a visit.

The city of Amsterdam repaid Victor Kugler's visit to the site of the Secret Annex at the highest level, in Toronto.

On May 8, 1975, Amsterdam Mayor Ivo Samkalden spoke in Toronto, where he accepted the Brotherhood Award from Congregation Beth Sholom on behalf of the citizens of the Dutch capital, and met one of Amsterdam's most distinguished former residents, Victor Kugler. At the time, Congregation Beth Sholom's spiritual leader was Rabbi David Monson, who remains one of North America's leading Jewish clerics and is a major fund-raiser for Jerusalem's Shaarei Tzedek Hospital. According to the *Toronto Star*, Rabbi Monson paid tribute to the "sympathy and solidarity citizens of the Netherlands showed for the Jewish population" during World War II:

> For Samkalden, it was a chance to meet Victor Kugler. Kugler praised Toronto where he said he had found a great deal of friendship, with all colours, races and creeds living together harmoniously. Samkalden said the sacrifices made by the Canadian soldiers who liberated the Netherlands would be enshrined in the hearts of its citizens forever. "Thirty years have passed since the end of the war, but the Canadian graves are still tended by the people."

Victor Kugler's memoirs as told to Eda Shapiro continue:

> Nor does interest in Anne Frank flag. Recently, a book has been published, called *Weerklank van Anne Frank*. Translated, that means "Echo of Anne Frank." Mr. Frank has kindly sent me a copy. The book contains touching tributes to the memory of his daughter. People from all corners of the world express their feelings in their native languages, and in their own fashion. Their emotions are reflected in letters, poems, paintings, statues and music. Each tribute shows the profound effect her diary has had on different people.
>
> I was very touched when I read Mr. Frank's inscription, in German, on the flyleaf of this book:
>
>> Herr Kugler zur Erinnerung an alles, was er für mich und meine Familie wahrend unserer Untertauchzeit getan hat.
>>
>> In alter Verbundenheit,
>> Otto Frank
>> April 26, 1970
>
> Translated it says:
>
>> To Mr. Kugler, in remembrance of everything he did for me and my family during the time we were in hiding.
>>
>> With sincere friendship bound together,
>> Otto Frank
>
> As for Mr. Kleiman (the Mr. Koophuis of Anne's diary), he unfortunately is now gone. In the diary, Anne made several references to his stomach troubles. I have also kept in touch with Miep and Elli, the office girls who helped out. I have a letter from Miep, enclosing a clipping from an Amsterdam newspaper. She knows how fond I am of music. The clipping was about a famous conductor who was visiting Amsterdam, and whose work Miep knew I admired.

Oskar Morawetz's From the Diary of Anne Frank

Shortly after Victor Kugler retired, Oskar Morawetz's epic symphonic and vocal composition *From the Diary of Anne Frank* received its world premiere

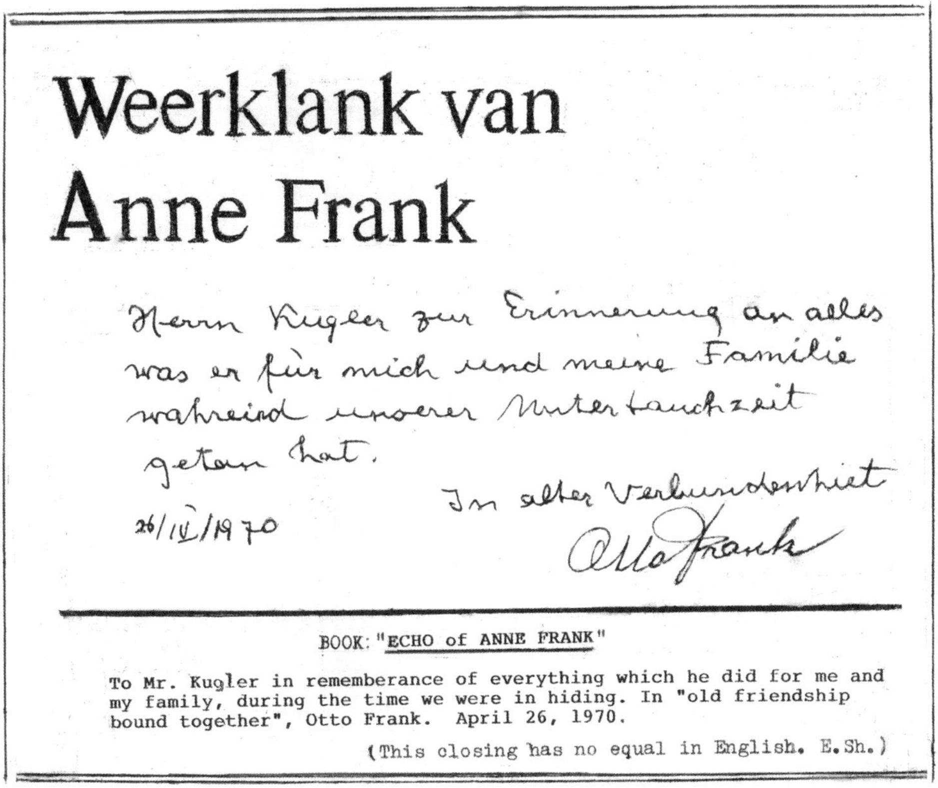

Weerklank van Anne Frank

[handwritten German inscription]

Herrn Kugler zur Erinnerung an alles was er für mich und meine Familie während unserer Untertauchzeit getan hat.

26/IV/1970

In alter Verbundenheit
Otto Frank

BOOK: "ECHO of ANNE FRANK"

To Mr. Kugler in rememberance of everything which he did for me and my family, during the time we were in hiding. In "old friendship bound together", Otto Frank.   April 26, 1970.

(This closing has no equal in English. E.Sh.)

Otto Frank's inscription on the flyleaf of Echo of Anne Frank *(courtesy of Victor Kugler)*

by the Toronto Symphony at Toronto's Massey Hall, an acoustically perfect Victorian auditorium which is Canada's equivalent of Carnegie Hall. This was at a time when the Toronto Symphony was at its peak as an orchestra of world stature. Its conductor, Karel Ancerl, had conducted the first performance of the Jewish-composed opera *Brundibar* in 1944 in the Nazi concentration camp at Theresienstadt. The opera's composer and performers were all murdered at Auschwitz soon after its premiere. Mr. Ancerl led the Czech Philharmonic until the Soviet invasion of 1968 forced him to leave his homeland. Many of the Toronto Symphony's musicians were Soviet Jewish émigrés. The soprano who sang the excerpts from the diary was Lois Marshall, who was Canada's leading opera singer at the time. Otto Frank attended the performance, and gave flowers to Ms. Marshall. It can be argued that this premiere was one of the greatest musical events in Canada's history. Among those present was Victor Kugler. Oskar Morawetz told me how he met Mr. Kugler:

> I had been in contact with Otto Frank during the composition of *From the Diary of Anne Frank,* and Mr. Frank wrote to me from Amsterdam to inform me that Victor Kugler lived in Toronto. That is how I established contact.
>
> When he first visited me at my house, his English was slow. He spoke German better than English. He always arrived beautifully dressed, wearing a tie. Mr. Kugler was extremely helpful, but he was extremely modest. At social gatherings, even when the Holocaust was mentioned, he would never discuss his role in hiding Anne Frank. Only when the topic of Anne Frank was directly brought up did he say, very shyly, "Well, I hid Anne Frank."
>
> But when people directly asked him about his role in hiding Anne Frank, Victor Kugler was very cooperative and very helpful. He was very generous in giving me pictures and copies of pictures.
>
> He had a big box of photos and memorabilia of his life. In this box was a New Year's card that Anne Frank had sent him, before she and her family had to hide. Realizing the immense value of this card, I said, "Mr. Kugler, you should have it locked up." Victor was quite surprised. I asked him, "Could we go to a photocopying store and make ten copies?" Victor Kugler did so.
>
> Later, when I asked him if I could look at it again, he told me that he had presented it as a gift to Rabbi Dr. David Monson who had sent it to its current *resting place*: the Israel Museum in Jerusalem.
>
> Another composition of mine, also based on the text of the *diary,* was performed at Toronto's Temple Sinai in the 1970s, shortly after the major diary work was premiered at Massey Hall. The text was based on the passage in the *diary,* "Who has allowed us to suffer so terribly up until now?"
>
> It was sung by Temple Sinai Cantor Severin Weingort, under the musical direction of Ben Steinberg [*also one of Canada's most prominent Jewish composers — ed.*]. After this concert, I told the audience, "I have a big surprise. Mr. Kugler lives in Toronto and he is present at this performance."

Hardly anybody who attended this concert knew that he lived in their hometown. When they heard this, people were so excited that they got down on their knees as though a biblical prophet had come.

Then Victor Kugler was asked to say a few words. This was the first time he had ever publicly spoken to an audience at an occasion meant to honor him. Oskar Morawetz recounts: "He was very shy and said a few words. But they were not about him. They were words of praise about Otto Frank."

Cantor Weingort said, "Meeting Mr. Victor Kugler in person makes one believe in mankind."

New Friends and Connections

At the reception following the Massey Hall premiere of Oskar Morawetz's *From the Diary of Anne Frank*, Victor and Lucy Kugler were introduced to Jacobus and Berthe Nunes-Vaz, descendants of a Sephardic-Jewish family that had played a prominent role in Spain prior to the Inquisition. Following the expulsion of the Jews from Spain in 1492, the family had settled in the Netherlands. After this introduction, the Nunes-Vazes formed a warm friendship with the Kuglers. Here are some of their memories:

> Shortly after we met the Kuglers, we realized that they were living in financially restrained circumstances. Lucy was a bookkeeper. I hired her for my diamond importing business.
>
> We became very close friends. They were always welcome at our home in the Post Road district [*Toronto's wealthiest residential area — ed.*] and we had many good times together. But they were very reluctant to discuss his past.
>
> We celebrated Victor Kugler's seventy-fifth birthday in our home. Together with Murray Koffler, James Kay and Morris Kerzner [*some of Toronto's, and for that matter Canada's, most prominent Jewish corporate citizens and philanthropists — ed.*], we managed to send him to Israel, where he planted a tree on the Avenue of the Righteous Gentiles at Israel's Holocaust memorial, Yad Vashem.

How Victor Kugler came to be so honored by Yad Vashem as a Righteous

Gentile and some details of this trip to Israel will be described in detail in the next chapter.

The Nunes-Vazes report that at the time of his birthday celebration, Victor, who, according to Rita Visser, had previously been in excellent health, being an adherent of holistic medicine, began to show signs, at times, of losing his memory. He had begun to develop Alzheimer's disease.

Reaching Out in the Community

Oskar Morawetz helped Victor Kugler publicize his role in sheltering Anne Frank in other ways besides featuring him at performances of his own musical works. During the early 1970s, Evelyn Wolfe had a TV show on the then-new Toronto Rogers Cable station. Mr. Morawetz suggested that she interview Victor Kugler, which she did. Although she had, by chance, sat next to Mr. Kugler during the Royal Alexandra performance of the play, at the time she did not know who he really was, and therefore did not resume contact until Morawetz suggested it.

Two significant highlights of the TV interview include Victor Kugler's discussion of his numerous speeches to schools in Toronto and his feelings towards Holland and the Germans:

> A few days ago I got an invitation from a school in Willowdale [*a comfortable suburban neighborhood in northern metro Toronto — ed.*]. I often receive such invitations. I am astonished how interested today's kids are in the story of Anne Frank.

During the early 1970s, Victor Kugler was invited to speak about his wartime experiences at several high schools in Toronto. He was greeted as a hero. Perhaps the most important and moving high school tribute came from a student named Sharon O'Grady, who addressed a touching poem to Victor Kugler on behalf of the Grade 10 students at St. Joseph's High School, a Catholic parochial school in the Islington district of Toronto's far west end. The school has no Jewish presence whatsoever, yet the students were visibly moved by his presentation. Indeed, Victor Kugler was recognized as a hero throughout the entire Canadian population, transcending all religious borders.

During those early 1970s, Victor Kugler also spoke at Markham District

High School in the rapidly growing upscale northeastern Toronto suburb of Markham, where the ethnic makeup was and remains very diverse. He also spoke at B'nai Brith lodges, not only in Toronto, but also in Chatham. Chatham is a southwestern Ontario town of about sixty thousand with a substantial Afro-Canadian population whose ancestors came from the United States during the slave era via the Underground Railroad. The *Chatham Free Press* mentioned:

> Mr. Kugler told Chatham B'nai Brith Thursday night (September 21, 1972) he didn't tell his wife of this nerve-wracking attempt to save the family of his business partner because it would be too dangerous for her.

But during those years in the 1970s, Victor Kugler saved his most intimate and heartfelt comments for Eda Shapiro and Evelyn Wolfe. When Mrs. Wolfe interviewed him on TV, he said:

> I have no desire to return to Holland to live, as I have no family in Holland.
>
> I don't like the Germans. The Germans are very adamant and demanding. They are superbly disciplined technicians. They should keep those attitudes to those things. They play soldier but they don't win wars.

The TV interview was the beginning of a long and mutually rewarding friendship between the Wolfes and the Kuglers. As Mrs. Wolfe said:

> We became very friendly with the Kuglers. He was very bright. He would talk about geography, history, and photography. Following his retirement, we did everything we could to help them. Our friend Louis Mayzel helped them too. He bought them a fridge and linoleum, and sent them to Israel, a trip that they greatly enjoyed.
>
> The Jewish community in Toronto has been very supportive of the Kuglers. Various rabbis have honored his presence in this city.
>
> In 1974, Victor Kugler visited Otto Frank in Amsterdam. The Kuglers had a lovely time. He told Otto Frank about Evelyn Wolfe, and her interest in what he would call "the Story" (the Secret Annex period and afterwards).

He received various honors both at home and abroad [*more of these in the next chapter — ed.*] and in 1980 he spoke at the Toronto Jewish Book Fair [*North America's oldest and still largest annual event of this type — ed.*].

But it is also true that late in his life, Mr. Kugler suffered occasional time lapses. The Kuglers would visit us fairly frequently. Once, he said to us, "I want to go to Utrecht." He thought that our house on Robinwood Avenue was like Utrecht. So then, when they came to us, he knew that he was in Utrecht, Holland.

And then, just before he died, Victor and Lucy Kugler were at our house, when, without warning, he went up the stairs.

Lucy said, "Where are you going, Victor?"

To which Victor replied, "I'm just going upstairs to check that the people are all right."

Chapter Nine

Honors — Yad Vashem

On the pine-covered western hillsides overlooking Jerusalem, bordering Mount Herzl, Israel's most important military cemetery, there is a massive, sleekly modern, cream-colored Jerusalem stone monument to the six million Jews murdered by Hitler. This edifice is called Yad Vashem, the Holocaust Martyrs's and Heroes' Remembrance Authority.

Perhaps as a reaction to the flowery artistic romanticism favored by Hitler, the Nazis, and many other European anti-Semites, the dominant characteristic of Yad Vashem is that of a stark, contemporary functional simplicity. One enters a museum that presents a graphic photographic history of the rise of the Third Reich, culminating with the ghettos, mobile shooting squads (Einsatzgruppen) and extermination camps. The climax of the exhibit is a large room with the eternal flame in memory of the six million. The names of the death camps, written in both Latin and Hebrew characters, are inscribed around the flame.

All of this is inside. Outside, alongside the windowless edifice, bathed by the brilliant sunlight that shines on Jerusalem three-fourths of the year and soaked by the rain and snow of winter, is the Avenue of the Righteous Gentiles. This cream-colored Jerusalem stone walkway, which ascends a hill, is lined on both sides by hundreds of plaques. Each of them bears the name of a Gentile in occupied Europe who personally risked his or her life to save a Jew.

The memorialized Righteous Gentiles hail from Germany and every country in occupied Europe. The two countries with the highest number of Righteous Gentiles are Poland and Holland. The population of Poland was six times larger than that of Holland, but the Jewish death rate in Holland

(75 percent) was nearly as high as that of Poland (90 percent). In this context, the proportion of Righteous Gentiles in the Netherlands was the highest in any Nazi-occupied European country.

Righteous among the Nations

To become recognized as a Righteous Gentile, whether one is alive or dead, is no simple procedure. The following memoirs of Eda Shapiro reveal her efforts to secure this immortal honor for Victor Kugler while he was still alive.

> I realized that this book about Victor Kugler is not only about one of the people who hid Anne Frank. It is also about a Righteous Gentile. Indeed, in my opinion, this book records part of the chronicle of a whole nation of Righteous Gentiles — the Dutch people. I therefore resolved that Mr. Victor Kugler deserved to be honored as a Righteous Gentile. Consequently, on March 2, 1971, I wrote to Yad Vashem Holocaust Martyrs' and Heroes' Remembrance Authority, Israel, recommending that he be awarded the Medal of the Righteous.
>
> On August 19, 1953, Israel's Knesset (Parliament) passed the Martyrs' and Heroes' Remembrance Law, under which the Yad Vashem Remembrance Authority was set up in Jerusalem. Some of the authority's functions include the commemoration of the Holocaust's victims, their communities, organizations and institutions, and the rebels and fighters who rose up against the enemy in defense of the people's honor.
>
> The Yad Vashem compound was built on the Mount of Remembrance, near Mount Herzl, in the western part of Jerusalem. A Pillar of Heroism was erected there in honor of the resistance fighters, together with a Hall of Remembrance museum and a synagogue, a permanent exhibition, a hall of names, and a separate building to house the archives, the library and the administration offices.
>
> My letter to Yad Vashem reads in part as follows:
>
>> I have already pointed out how strongly I feel about recording as much as possible about the Holocaust, preferably through

the eyes and minds of the victims, as in my book *Tales of the Holocaust* by the survivors. At the same time, I feel that the world should know about the Righteous Gentiles — the people who were so wonderful to my Jewish brethren. I know that Yad Vashem honors such Gentiles with the Medal of the Righteous. The purpose of this letter and enclosed material is to respectfully suggest that Mr. Victor Kugler, who risked his life to hide Anne Frank, her family, and four others, in the hope of saving their lives, surely deserves to be honored with the Medal of the Righteous.

On April 28, 1971, Eda Shapiro received this written reply from Yad Vashem:

Dear Madame:

I thank you for your letter of March 2nd and the material enclosed, which was delivered to us by the Israeli Consulate in Toronto.

We shall do everything necessary to bring about the recognition of Mr. Kugler as a Righteous Gentile by the Commission for the Righteous. The commission functions according to formal procedures, one of which is that testimonies must come directly from the Jews saved.

Accordingly, we shall contact Mr. Otto Frank and ask him for all the information concerning Mr. Kugler. In due time we shall inform you of the outcome of the matter. In the meantime I shall thank you kindly for all you have done to bring that matter to our attention.

Sincerely,
Shalmi Barmore
Department for the Righteous

P.S. I was very much surprised to receive a letter from Mr. Otto Frank, himself suggesting we honor all those who helped the family, including Mr. Kugler.

Eda Shapiro describes what happened next:

The next letter I received from Yad Vashem was written in Hebrew, and addressed to me in Jerusalem. (In the interim, my family and I

YAD VASHEM   רשות־הזיכרון לשואה ולגבורה   **יד ושם**
                    MARTYRS' & HEROES' REMEMBRANCE AUTHORITY

JERUSALEM, HAR HAZIKARON (P.O.B. 84) – CABLES, YADVASHEM – TEL. 31307   ירושלים, הר הזיכרון, (ת"ד 84) – מברקים: ירושם – טל. 31307.

Jerusalem, 28th April, 1971

Mrs. Eda Shapiro
3892 Bathurst St., Apt. 307
Downsview, Ontario, <u>Canada</u>

Re: <u>Mr. Kugler, Victor - Holland (Canada)</u>

Dear Madame,

    I thank you for your letter of March 2nd, and the material
enclosed, which was delivered to us by the Israeli Consulate in
Toronto.

    We shall do everything necessary to bring about the recogni-
tion of Mr. Kugler as a Righteous Gentile, by the Commission for the
Righteous. The Commission functions according to formal procedures-
one of which is that testimonies must come directly from the Jews saved.

    Accordingly, we shall contact Mr. Otto Frank and ask him for
all the information concerning Mr. Kugler. In due time we shall inform
you of the outcome of the matter.

    In the meantime, I thank you kindly for all you have done to
bring that matter to our attention.

                                          Sincerely,

                                          Shalmi Barmore

                                          Shalmi Barmore
                                          Department for the Righteous.

P.S. - I was very much surprised to receive a letter from Otto Frank,
       himself suggesting we honour all those who helped his family,
       including Mr. Kugler.

A letter from Yad Vashem to Eda Shapiro regarding her request to recognize Mr. Kugler
as a Righteous Gentile (courtesy of Eda Shapiro)

had moved to Israel from Canada in 1971.) This Hebrew letter I have translated as follows:

> YAD VASHEM HOLOCAUST MARTYRS' AND HEROES'
> REMEMBRANCE AUTHORITY
> Jerusalem, March 19, 1972
>
> Subject: Victor Kugler and others: Holland
>
> Dear Mrs. Shapiro:
>
> I am pleased to inform you that the Commission for the Righteous decided in its meeting of March 8, 1972, to award the above, under separate cover, the highest symbol of esteem, a medal, plus the right to plant a tree (in the Avenue of the Righteous).
>
> The honor will be given to the saviors by means of our embassies in one of their coming dispatches.
>
> Sincerely,
> (signed) Mrs. Donia Rosen

I have had the privilege of holding this medal and examining it and I should like to describe it. It was struck specially for Yad Vashem by the Israel Government Coins and Medals Corporation. The medallion, made of silver, is encased in an olivewood box lined with dark blue velvet. On the right side of the box top, in silver, is the emblem of Israel, the seven-branched candelabrum. A tiny silver clasp opens and closes it.

Nathan Karp, the designer, inscribed on it the Talmudic saying "He who saves a single life, saves the whole world." This is on both sides, in French and Hebrew. One shows two skeleton hands in concentration camp garb, reaching out beyond for world freedom. The other shows Yad Vashem, the hills above it, and a carob tree, a "thank you" from the Jewish people, and the recipient's name.

On April 5, 1973, at the Israeli consulate in Toronto, Shmuel Ovnat, who was then the consul general of Israel, presented Victor Kugler with the Medal of the Righteous, as recommended by Otto Frank and Eda Shapiro.

In 1975, when he went to Israel, Victor Kugler visited Yad Vashem and saw his name inscribed on a plaque under a tree, planted in his honor, on the Avenue of the Righteous Gentiles.

Jacobus and Berthe Nunes-Vaz provided the following memories of the ceremony honoring Victor Kugler at Yad Vashem:

> Many Israeli dignitaries, especially Teddy Kollek [*the venerable long-serving mayor of Jerusalem — ed.*], personally honored Victor Kugler. But, characteristic of his extreme humility, he was annoyed by the constant publicity he received in Israel. He complained that he had no rest.
>
> Lucy, who herself came from a humble Dutch background, said: "We didn't want these honors."
>
> But Victor Kugler was by no means ungrateful. He had his own special way of showing just how much being cited as a Righteous Gentile meant to him.
>
> When he planted the tree on the Avenue of the Righteous Gentiles, he picked its tiniest leaf and wore it on his lapel until the day he died.

In 1979, Victor Kugler's memoirs were published by Yad Vashem.

Honors in Toronto

It has often been said that the greatest recognition is to be recognized at home, especially in cities such as Toronto where visiting dignitaries take precedence over local celebrities.

Such spotlight recognition came to Victor Kugler in his home city during the last decade of his life, in the form of a Foundation financial award, a performance of *From the Diary of Anne Frank* in Beth Tikvah Congregation where he was the guest of honor, a documentary by an internationally acclaimed TV producer, and, finally, a civic affair in which he and Canada's most famous foreign diplomat of the late 1970s were honored together for their heroism.

Awarded by the Canadian Council of Christians and Jews

In 1977, at a banquet in Toronto's most famous hotel, the Royal York, in the heart of the financial district, the Canadian Council of Christians and Jews presented Victor Kugler with the Nicholas and Hedy Munk Brotherhood Award of ten thousand dollars for hiding the Franks, the van Pelses and Friedrich Pfeffer in the Secret Annex.

(The Munk family is one of Canada's leading business families. The son of Nicholas and Hedy, Peter, is one of Canada's most influential corporate executives. In 1972, through the Munk charitable trust, a sum of money was set aside that yields ten thousand dollars every second year. The money is awarded to a man or woman anywhere in the world who has promoted understanding.)

How the modest Victor Kugler received this prestigious award is described in a letter written by the late prominent Toronto Jewish communal official Ben Kayfetz, who until his passing in the late 1990s delivered a weekly radio column on Canadian Jewish news and views. This letter was dated September 8, 1996:

> At some point in the late 1970s, I received a phone call from Charles Wittenberg (since deceased). I was then executive director of Canadian Jewish Congress, Ontario Region.
>
> Mr. Wittenberg was known to me as a veteran of the French *Resistance* and an activist in countering neo-Nazis in Toronto.
>
> What Mr. Wittenberg was calling about was the case of Victor Kugler, the benefactor of Anne Frank. This man, who sheltered her family from the Nazis, was living in the Toronto area and was in dire straits financially. Could I help, either through Canadian Jewish Congress or in some other way?
>
> I consulted with Rabbi Jordan Pearlson, then national chairman of the Canadian Jewish Congress Community Relations Committee. I chose to speak to him first because I thought he would know his way around in the community and knew which buttons to push.
>
> My guess was right on target. Rabbi Pearlson immediately proposed giving him the Nicholas Munk award. This had been set up several years earlier by Nicholas Munk to be awarded every other year to the person who had done most to build interreligious and interracial harmony. The amount given was ten thousand dollars. Rabbi Pearlson made a few phone calls to persons on the award

committee whom he knew and all agreed that Mr. Kugler would be an appropriate selection.

I visited the Kuglers about this time at their home in Weston at 22 Braeburn Avenue. I still have the address in my listings. I recall that Charles Wittenberg was there. He arranged the meeting. I don't recall whether or not (Rabbi) Jordan Pearlson was present.

Unfortunately, there was no way I could carry on a conversation with Mr. Kugler. He was in his late seventies and had been afflicted with some kind of stroke and seemed to have lost part of his speech. Most of the talking was done by his wife Lucy. She was not a direct witness to the events as they married after the war, I understand.

Even so, the result of this meeting was the belated recognition of Victor Kugler as a shining beacon of heroism, recognized in one of the most prestigious arenas in the heart of North America's second-largest financial center.

The awards dinner was conducted in the grandest tradition of Toronto high society events at the time. There was an air of British-style pomp and formal dignity. Of course, this formal atmosphere was the only appropriate manner in which to honor Victor Kugler. Most of Canada's leading corporate executives and their wives were present.

He was escorted in to the awards dinner by Grade 11 student Jill Daffern from Malvern Collegiate, a school in the trendy Beaches area of Toronto's east side which is far removed, both geographically and spiritually, from the traditional Jewish areas. After she pushed in his chair she kissed him on the cheek.

The *Toronto Star's* Michael McAteer described the proceedings:

> Rabbi Michael Stroh, president of the Toronto Board of Rabbis, called Kugler's wartime deed an "act of pure moral courage."
>
> Stroh noted that Anne Frank had written in her diary that despite the evil around her she still believed in the "good in people." Kugler's actions, Stroh said, underlined this belief.

Rabbi Stroh later commented on his personal experience as he made the presentation to Victor Kugler:

> When I introduced Victor Kugler, I commented on his statement that he hid the people as he did because, morally, he had no choice. It did not occur to him to do otherwise. I reflected on those people who

find doing the moral thing ordinary even when it is an extraordinary act of courage.

After the presentation, Kugler said that he had been "too moved" to reply. "I could not find the words."

It was left to Claus van Banning, vice-consul of the Netherlands, to help explain why Kugler risked his life to save the Jews.

"'They were my friends' is how Kugler answers," van Banning said. "'What could I do?'"

Victor Kugler was the third recipient of the Nicholas and Hedy Munk Brotherhood Award.

The CBC-TV Documentary Film

Shortly afterwards, Harry Rasky of the Canadian Broadcasting Corporation, one of Canada's best recognized documentary TV producers, produced a film on the life of Victor Kugler, entitled *The Man Who Hid Anne Frank*. This hour-long film was seen not only throughout Canada but also on public networks around the world.

Victor Kugler was also an honored guest on what was then Canada's most-watched news-interview TV program, the CBC's *Front Page Challenge*. There, he was asked questions by a panel of Canada's leading TV-radio journalists of the 1970s and early 1980s: Pierre Berton, Gordon Sinclair, Betty Kennedy and Fred Davis.

"To Be Awarded Together with Ken Taylor"

But perhaps the climactic Canadian tribute to Victor Kugler took place on June 10, 1980, the year before his death, at a civic luncheon in the metro Toronto City of North York.

In 1997, the Ontario provincial government amalgamated its six boroughs into one large city called Toronto. Mel Lastman (who had previously served as the mayor of North York, which was one of these boroughs) was elected the first mayor of this new big city; he retired in 2004.

Even his foes concede him to be reasonably honest and immensely popular. He is demonstrably proud of his Jewish heritage and has continually lent his name to numerous Israeli and domestic Jewish causes. Mel thinks big, and when he decides to lend his name to any form of ceremony, it is guaranteed to be a Big Event.

And so it was when Victor Kugler was honored alongside Ken Taylor, the Canadian ambassador to Iran who, in the early and fanatic days of the Ayatollah's regime, hid six American diplomats in the Canadian embassy in Teheran and then clandestinely smuggled them out. This was the first formal affair in Canada to honor Taylor, so many leading politicians from all over the nation were in attendance as well as all of the local mayors and Toronto's Metro Chairman Paul Godfrey (now president of the *Toronto Sun* and CEO of the Toronto Blue Jays major league baseball team).

The *Toronto Star*'s Warren Potter wrote up a fairly large article on this civic luncheon at the Montecassino Place hotel. Some relevant excerpts:

> Lastman, in emotional speeches, praised the courage of both Taylor and Kugler.
>
> He said Taylor and his staff had shown the world that Canada and Canadians have spirit, courage and cunning.
>
> "Your story is filled with daring and intrigue and heroics," he told Taylor. "You were called to perform a humanitarian act and you rose to the occasion without hesitation and did not falter."
>
> There was an even more emotional atmosphere among the audience, many of them Jewish, when Lastman praised Kugler for his bravery.
>
> Kugler hid Anne Frank, whose account of her life in the attic was published after her death and became a bestseller, *The Diary of Anne Frank*.
>
> Kugler was shipped to a labor camp but escaped and made his way back to Holland.
>
> Lastman said Kugler demonstrated generosity, bravery and a persistent belief in doing his humanitarian duty, regardless of personal cost.
>
> "This is his legacy to the world and it will never be forgotten," Lastman said. "We look back, in security and comfort, and say, 'Thank God for Victor Kugler,' and people like him who knew their duty and did it.

"Yet most of us cannot know the depths of courage that he had to call upon to harbor those eight people when the streets below echoed with the gunshots of the Nazis and the cries of Jews being tortured and being led to death camps.

"Words and awards are not really adequate to thank Kugler for what he did," Lastman said.

"As a Jew I feel a very special gratitude. As mayor of North York I am proud that you have made Canada your home."

Special awards were also made to Taylor and Kugler by Sam Filer, chairman of the national executive office of the Canadian Jewish Congress.

Inscriptions on the framed scrolls read, as quoted from the Jewish Talmud: "Whosoever preserves a single soul, it is as if he preserved the whole world."

Chapter Ten

Conclusion

Eva Shapiro recorded in her notes:

> Sometimes, he goes down to Toronto's lakefront and stares at the Lancaster plane anchored there. "I am always glad. It is the same when I see a Spitfire in a magazine."
>
> And now, after all that life, how is his health?
>
> "Fine," he says. "I've never been sick a day in my life."

Victor Kugler died on December 16, 1981, at the age of eighty-one, at Etobicoke General Hospital, in Toronto's west end, of complications resulting from Alzheimer's disease.

Farewell to a Hero

The following description of the funeral was compiled from information found in the *Toronto Star* and the *Canadian Jewish News* coverage of the event.

It was a small funeral at the tiny Ward Funeral Home on Weston Road, more than twelve miles northwest of downtown Toronto.

Among the one hundred mourners who packed the funeral service was a sixty-year-old interior designer who wiped away tears as a rabbi and minister spoke.

"He wouldn't know me," said the North York man, "but I was in a concentration camp in Czechoslovakia."

"Victor Kugler could never understand the honors given to him," said Rabbi Jordan Pearlson of Temple Sinai, where Victor Kugler was guest of honor for an Oskar Morawetz composition dedicated to Anne Frank eleven years before.

Rabbi Pearlson said that Kugler used to say, "I don't understand what all the fuss is all about."

The rabbi added that because of Victor Kugler, "There is more than ashes; there is a book — a child's voice that cries out and says 'remember.'"

Reverend Victor Wood of Westway United Church, who conducted the service in the Ward Funeral Home, praised Kugler as a man of many talents who studied languages, was an amateur photographer, and enjoyed addressing school children.

"He was not forgotten by his own people or by the Jewish community, and that is a great tribute," said Reverend Wood.

Present was the Dutch consul general, Tom Kasteel, and Israeli consul general David Ariel. Numerous members of the clergy attended the funeral.

As the casket was removed from the funeral home, eleven men from the Jewish War Veterans and the General Wingate Branch of the Canadian Legion formed an honor guard.

The Life of Lucy Kugler Just before and after Victor's Death

"She was an energetic, beautiful lady."

So said a longtime friend, Dr. Claire Nunes-Vaz of Toronto, daughter of Jacobus and Berthe Nunes-Vaz, in regards to Lucy Kugler.

According to her sister, Rita Visser: "Lucy was very outgoing. Victor and Lucy had lots of friends. She was a Leo and had a nice personality."

But even before her husband's death, the quality of life, both physically and economically, began to deteriorate for Lucy Kugler. Because Victor Kugler had worked as a self-employed commissioned insurance salesman all of his time in Canada, he received no company pension. The Canadian Registered Retirement Savings Plan, which primarily benefits self-employed business individuals and professionals, was only initiated in the early 1970s, shortly after he retired. So it was of no benefit to either him or Lucy. There were only Lucy's earnings as a bookkeeper for the Nunes-Vazes to pay the household bills after Victor retired. The Kuglers, while they were never impoverished and owned their house free and clear, nonetheless had no independent savings for their old age. For whatever reason, they had no matured life insurance benefits either. All Lucy had to live on were the newly initiated Canadian Old Age Security Pension and the benefits from the Canada Pension Plan, which was then in its infancy. The Guaranteed Income Supplement, which is now a part of Canadian Old Age Security payments, did not begin until the mid-1970s.

According to Oskar Morawetz, who maintained close contact with the Kuglers right up until Victor's death, and with Lucy in the ten years until she too died, Lucy's life with Victor in the last year was very strenuous, because he had lost his mental capacities. The twenty-seven-year age difference between the Kuglers aggravated the situation during his last year. Yet, the Kuglers' relationship remained basically happy and loving up until the end. After he died, she told Oskar that she wished she could have him back so that she could continue to take care of him.

Following Victor's death, Lucy's own health deteriorated. She developed terminal cancer. She had constant operations, and due to radiation therapy, she lost her hair. Emotionally, according to Rita Visser: "She was lost after Victor's death. She was always talking about Victor."

According to Rita Visser, in the three years before Victor's death, when his health had begun to deteriorate, the Kuglers moved to a second Weston house which they sold soon afterwards. They eventually ended up in a rented apartment in northwest metro Toronto, which provided Victor with a superb view of one of the beautiful wooded ravines that weave through the city. From a purely business viewpoint, the sale of their second house was a stroke of bad economic timing. Had the Kuglers held on to the second Weston house and had Lucy sold it a decade later, in the late 1980s when Toronto house prices had tripled due to a major infusion of Hong Kong money, she would have profited greatly. On the principal amount, with the high interest rates that prevailed throughout the 1980s, Lucy's last years could have been very financially secure. But for understandable reasons beyond their control, in the face of Victor's growing infirmity, the Kuglers did not wait to sell the second house. This was unfortunate.

Victor Kugler's close friends maintained contact with Lucy after Victor's death. Lucy, although not Jewish, continued to maintain a strong interest in Jewish and Holocaust topics.

In the mid-1980s, Oskar Morawetz took Lucy Kugler to see the German-made movie *The Wannsee Conference*, which recreated the January 20, 1942, conference that sealed the fate of European Jewry. At that ornate villa in the West Berlin suburb of Wannsee, SD chief Reinhard Heydrich chaired a ninety-minute conference, attended by Adolf Eichmann and other Nazi bigwigs (although not by Adolf Hitler himself), which decreed that all Jews living in German-controlled territory be exterminated. The only point of contention amongst the twenty-odd attendants was whether or not people whose ancestry was less than one-fourth Jewish should be included in the mass death sentence. The debate was accompanied by sarcastic remarks and other attempts at cheap, macabre humor. The entire movie was a recreation of this conference. Nothing else was included.

Oskar Morawetz recounted that this movie left Lucy Kugler "very shocked."

Despite such frequent overtures of friendship, according to Dr. Morawetz, Lucy Kugler's physical and economic situation continued to deteriorate progressively as the 1980s wore on.

She died of cancer on June 8, 1991, nearly ten years after the death of her husband.

The Kuglers' Final Resting Place

Victor and Lucy Kugler are both buried at Riverside Cemetery in Toronto's west end. The burial site is plain and simple. Until he was informed, the present director of the cemetery, John Barrett, had no idea who Victor Kugler was. As he wrote in a letter to Irving Naftolin, Eda Shapiro's second husband:

> From all the information you have given me, I can see that the late Victor Kugler was an important man, and a light for humanity at a dark time in our history.
>
> I have no more information that would add to your knowledge of this man, except that I can answer your question: should Mr. Kugler have had a stone? There is a memorial bronze marker on the lot for the late Victor and Lucy Kugler. I enclose a photograph of this marker for your records.

But there remains no tombstone.

Epilogue

The life and death of Victor Kugler fits remarkably into the general pattern of Righteous Gentile identified by Nechama Tec, associate professor of sociology at the University of Stamford in Connecticut, in her authoritative study of the subject, *When Light Pierced the Darkness*. Although her study refers to Poland during the Holocaust, there are illustrative parallels to the Netherlands because the Jewish death rate was nearly as high there.

Generally speaking, Righteous Gentiles, who risked their lives to shelter Jews, came from all classes and occupational backgrounds. Some were political activists; many were not. It is true that some Gentiles shielded Jews for monetary gain. Cynics can argue that Victor Kugler fitted into that category, because after all, he did acquire the Frank-owned Opekta business for free. But as Tec's study shows, the Gentiles who shielded Jews for monetary gain had a tendency to "take the money and run."

Once they received blood-payment, they either extorted more money from the helpless Jews or turned them over to the Nazis once they had been bled dry.

Obviously, Victor Kugler did not fit into this category. Even when he knew that the Secret Annex would be discovered after the burglary, he continued to do all he could to carry on as normal, protecting its inhabitants.

The uniting characteristics of Righteous Gentiles were rather to be found in their psychological profiles. There was a strong sense of individualism based on moral principle, whether it originated from actual friendship or on religious or other abstract, ethical humanist grounds. This was accompanied by modesty and disdain for personal aggrandizement. Dr. Tec's studies show that Victor Kugler's modest yet iron-willed personality and quiet sense of his own ethical responsibilities was the norm and not the exception.

What effect did the Righteous Gentiles have upon Hitler's all-powerful killing machine and its aftermath? Cynics can say: not much. On the other hand, there is the obvious example of Oskar Schindler; it is true that Raoul Wallenberg saved thousands of Hungarian Jews from deportation to Auschwitz; Sempo Sugihara, the Japanese envoy to Kovno, Lithuania, saved fifty thousand Jews by allowing them safe passage to Shanghai. And it is true that the legacy of Righteous Gentiles was generational in some cases. The German burgher Eberhard Helmrich sheltered Jews in his home during the 1930s and helped them emigrate. His daughter, Cornelia, who as a young child played with the children of the Jews he sheltered, is now Cornelia Schmalz-Jacobson. As leader of Germany's liberal Free Democratic Party and former minister of immigration in the Kohl coalition government, she was one of the most powerful forces combating neo-Nazi resurgences in Germany in the 1990s. While Germany continues to experience such racist outbreaks from time to time, they have not occurred on the same scale as in other European countries, and Ms. Schmalz-Jacobsen, daughter of a Righteous Gentile, although now retired, deserves much credit for setting an example of vigilance.

As for Victor Kugler, it can be said that his funeral, albeit modest, has left its own legacy of goodness. Christians and Jews united in a spontaneous tribute. His Toronto neighborhood of Weston is one of the most racially and economically integrated peaceful urban neighborhoods in any large North American city. While it is obvious that there is no direct cause and effect vis-à-vis the presence of Victor Kugler, it can be said that Victor Kugler's legacy has had a symbolic, positive effect on the environment in which he lived.

Obviously, it is paramount that the legacy of the Righteous Gentiles be much better publicized to combat Holocaust denial. Better publicity about the Righteous Gentiles' legacy would also provide an ethical example for the present and future in a world still plagued with racism and anti-Semitism. Whatever one may wish to say about Holland's role in the 1940s, it must be commended as the only continental European nation to stand up against the Arab oil embargo and boycott in the mid-1970s, the target of which was not just Israel but Jews around the world. The Dutch people cited the story of Anne Frank as the impetus behind this courageous lone stance.

Chroniclers of the Righteous Gentiles, such as Eda Shapiro, have begun to be appropriately recognized. In 1974, after reading the notes on Victor Kugler that have been compiled for this book, Otto Frank wrote to her from his home in Switzerland:

> Dear Mrs. Shapiro:
>
> As you can imagine, it took me some time to read your different letters to me, the clippings and the manuscript.
>
> As to the manuscript itself, I read it with great interest and think that it is written very well. The part connected with our hiding is related truthfully.
>
> Mr. Kugler told and wrote me much about his experiences, but in his detailed report are many facts I did not know and I must say that I was deeply moved learning about all the hardships he had to endure as a consequence of his help to us.
>
> I appreciate highly that your aim is to keep the terrible tragedy of the Holocaust alive, as well as the role of gentiles who helped their Jewish friends, and that therefore your wish is to get the memoirs of Mr. Kugler published.
>
> I am returning to you the manuscript and all the material you sent me by registered mail.
>
> Wishing you all the best, I am, with kind regards,
>
> Sincerely yours,
> Otto Frank

Otto Frank died in 1980 in Switzerland. Oskar Morawetz died in 2007 in Toronto.

In August 1982, Mark Shapiro returned to Toronto to continue his university studies. His father Sam died in Israel that same year, so Mark returned there for the funeral, bringing his mother, Eda, back to Toronto afterwards. She had always wanted to have her writings, interviews, and comments compiled in one book, *Tales of the Holocaust*.

In 1984, Eda met Irving Naftolin, and they married in 1986. In 1988, the *Toronto Sun* published a two-page spread of the memoirs of Victor Kugler as he had told them to her.

Miep Gies, upon whose memoirs Jon Blair based his award-winning documentary *Anne Frank Remembered*, in a letter written on her behalf by Cornelius Suijk, International Director for the Anne Frank Center USA in

New York, said she had read the memoirs "with great interest." She thanked Irving Naftolin for the courtesy of giving her access to these writings. In the letter, Mr. Suijk stated that Miep Gies "strongly supports the conviction that Victor Kugler, who was a truly good man, deserves to be remembered."

Rita Visser, who, as executor of Victor Kugler's estate owned a large number of his personal possessions, received numerous phone calls from people wanting to buy many of the items. Instead, In May 1995, she donated them to the Anne Frank House at the original site of the Secret Annex, Prinsengracht 263, Amsterdam, the Netherlands.

Eda Shapiro became ill with diabetes and suffered a stroke in 1990. She went into a nursing home, died in August 1992, and was buried in Israel.

Her husband, Irving Naftolin, says, "It is my pleasure to complete her work."

Appendix 1

Chronologies

A. *The Life of Victor Kugler*

1900 — Born in Austria.

1918 — Serves in Austrian navy.

1920-1933 — Works for bakery and spice company in Utrecht, Holland, as salesman.

1933-August 4, 1944 — Continues to work for Otto Frank, who has bought the company, now located in Amsterdam.

1934 — March — First meets Anne Frank. Parents and sister Margot have come before.

1942 — July 6 — Frank family goes into hiding in the Secret Annex of the third and fourth floor of the building. Four others come later.

1944 — August — Secret Annex discovered by Gestapo after being betrayed. All eight Jews and two managers — Victor Kugler and Jo Kleiman — sent to prison in Amsterdam and then on to three other prison camps: Amersfoort, Zwolle and Wageningen.

1945 — March — Victor Kugler escapes from big prison march to Germany. He gets home safely. His wife is sick. VE Day is May 7.

1955 — Victor Kugler moves to Toronto with second wife, Lucy, whose brother and sister live there. He becomes an insurance salesman and does well.

1958 — V.K. is invited by Leon Kossar to see play *Diary of Anne Frank* at Royal Alexander Theatre. It is "unnerving" to see himself portrayed.

1969 — V.K. lectures at Hebrew school of Eda Shapiro's son Mark. They meet and soon Eda starts a series of interviews with V.K. that continues for four years.

1970 — V.K. retires. He visits friends in Holland, and Otto Frank in Switzerland.

1973 — April 3 — In Toronto, V.K. receives Israel's "Righteous Medal" from Israeli consul general Shmuel Ovnat, with praise. It has been recommended by Eda Shapiro and Otto Frank.

1975 — V.K. plants a tree in Israel's "Garden of Righteous" at Yad Vashem.

1979 — The memoirs of V.K.'s experiences in German prison camps are published in Israel by Yad Vashem.

1980 — June 10 — V.K. is honored at an awards banquet by Council of Christians and Jews, with Ken Taylor, Canadian ambassador to Iran, who saved Americans. North York Mayor Mel Lastman presents them with "Key to North York" and his Mayor's Medal. The Hero of the 80s meets the Hero of the 40s.

1981 — Dec.16 — Victor Kugler dies at age 81. Buried in a Toronto cemetery with an honor guard of Toronto police and Jewish war veterans of 1900–1981.

1988 — October — Memoirs of Victor Kugler's wartime experiences are published in the *Toronto Sun* under the headline "The Man Who Hid Anne Frank."

1991 — Victor Kugler's second wife Lucy (1927–91) dies. Buried with him.

B. History of Victor Kugler Seen against Corresponding Events

1900 — Victor Kugler born in Austria.

1918 — Drafted into navy. Wounded and discharged with pension.

1918 — November 11 — World War I ends with armistice for Germany. Treaty of Versailles deals harsh terms for Germany.

1920 — Mr. Kugler moves to Utrecht, Holland, and lives there for 13 years. He becomes the manager of a bakery, restaurant, and a spice-importing business.

1928 — Travels to Belgium and Holland to increase business.

1929 — Anne Frank born. Her sister Margot is four years older.

1933 — Otto Frank moves to Amsterdam, Netherlands, from Frankfurt, Germany, to get away from anti-Semitic Germany. He buys the business of "Kolen & Co." and "Travis." The overall name is "Opekta." Mr. Kugler remains manager and becomes a friend. He moves to the Amsterdam suburb of Hilversum but works in Amsterdam.

1933 — Adolf Hitler becomes chancellor of Germany; in 1934, chief of army. He introduces anti-Semitic decrees and starts to round up Jews for concentration camps.

1938 — US President F.D. Roosevelt convenes the Evian Conference of the Western countries in France, to search for ways to save Jews. No country wants them.

1939 — September 1 — Germany invades Poland, conquering it in three weeks with planes, tanks and army (Blitzkrieg). No mercy for Jews.

1940 — Germany conquers Austria, Czechoslovakia, Belgium, Holland, France, Denmark and Norway. Holland's Queen Wilhelmina moves to exile in UK. Her daughter Princess Juliana moves to Ottawa, Canada, where she gives birth to Princess Beatrix.

1940 — April — Hitler appoints SS General Artur Seyss-Inquart Reichskommissar of Holland. Government is dissolved. Politicians, leaders and Jews sent to concentration camps. Discrimination decrees against Jews.

1941 — Unemployment and social unrest in Holland. On Feb. 25-26, dock workers and others go on strike to show friendship to Jews. Jews are herded into ghettos to work or be deported. In May, the Nuremburg Laws take effect in Holland: ID cards, fingerprints, Jews barred from cinemas and transportation. Jews must wear six-pointed Star of David made from yellow cloth.

1942 — January — The Wannsee Conference in Berlin. Aim: to build "work or die" concentration camps.

1942 — June — Anne Frank's 13th birthday. Among presents is her famous diary which she takes into hiding.

1942 — July — The Germans order Margot to report to a collection point to be shipped to Germany. The Franks hide in the now-famous house at

Prinsengracht 263. They are joined by three others — Mr. and Mrs. van Pels (known in the diary as van Daan) and son Peter, 15. Then Friedrich Pfeffer (Albert Dussel in the diary). Only Otto Frank survives.

1943 — April — Warsaw ghetto uprising.

1944 — August 4 — Hiding place discovered; betrayed by a worker. The eight people in it, together with Mr. Kugler and Mr. Kleiman, arrested by the Gestapo.

1944 — September — Kugler and Kleiman sent to Amersfoort forced labor camp. US planes bomb nearby railway tracks. Then, Kugler sent to Zwolle with about 600 men. The Germans organize manhunts for slave labor in Germany.

1944 — December — Anne and Margot sent to Bergen-Belsen.

1945 — January — Mrs. Edith Frank dies in Auschwitz.

1945 — February — Kugler sent to Wageningen forced labor camp. The commanding officer puts him in charge of the officers and workers, whom he helps.

1945 — March — Margot, then Anne, die in Bergen-Belsen.

1945 — March — Wageningen camp closed, and all have to march to Arnheim. Allied planes have bombed the tracks, and the railway men are on strike. Mr. Kugler and a friend escape on bicycles. With help of Dutch farmers, he arrives safely home in Hilversum, to find his wife sick.

1945 — May — Holland liberated from Germans by the Canadian Army two days before VE Day (May 8). German General Johannes Blaskowitz surrenders to Canadian General Foulks and HRH Prince Bernhardt of the Netherlands, in Wageningen, Holland.

1945 — summer — Otto Frank returns to Amsterdam and receives his daughter Anne's diary from office worker Miep Gies.

1952 — Victor Kugler's wife, Laura Kugler, dies. Three years later he marries Lucy van Langen.

1952 — Otto Frank moves to Basel, Switzerland.

1953 — November — Otto Frank marries Elfriede Geiringer.

1955 — Business not going well for V.K. Lucy has a brother in Toronto, Canada. Here Victor makes good as an insurance salesman.

1958 — Kugler attends play *Diary of Anne Frank* at Toronto's Royal Alexandra Theatre. He sees a recreation of what he did daily for over two years. This is painful. He resolves "never again" to see the play.

1959 — Johannes Kleiman dies on January 30.

1969 — Victor Kugler returns to Holland to visit friends. Then he goes to Switzerland to see Otto Frank. Frank is well, at age 80.

1969 — Eda Shapiro meets Kugler, and starts to interview him for his memoirs. This takes until approximately 1974. His memoirs of the forced labor camps are published by Yad Vashem in Jerusalem in 1979, and also in the *Toronto Sun* in 1988.

1971 — In February, the *Toronto Telegram* interviews Victor Kugler in his Toronto home. It is nicely furnished with pictures, a photographic darkroom, and a big map of the towns where he was in prison camps and those he fled through when he escaped. The main location is Prinsengracht 263: the business, warehouse, and Secret Annex.

1980 — August 19 — Otto Frank dies in Birsfelden, Switzerland, at the age of 91.

1981 — December 16 — Victor Kugler dies in Toronto, Canada, at the age of 81.

Appendix 2

A Letter of Tribute by Canada's Jewish War Veterans Commander, Sam Pasternak

With the outbreak of the Second World War on September 1, 1939, the civilized world was once again plunged into the cauldron of terror from which it would not be able to extricate itself for six long years.

This was to be a war such as humankind had never experienced. All the evil genius that the mind could devise, all the technological advances so painstakingly developed over the past quarter century, were to be directed towards ever greater and more fearful destruction. Death came on land, in the air, on the sea and under the sea. No one was safe. Military and civilian alike fell victim to the onslaught of the "Four Horsemen of the Apocalypse." Before this conflict ended about forty million people would be killed or murdered.

As evil as any war is, this one had an extra purpose and a special dimension: the complete murder and destruction of European Jewry. Aided and abetted by certain segments of local populations in various countries, the Nazis put six million Jews to death in the most horrifying manners imaginable. To be starved, beaten, experimented upon by deranged doctors, attacked and torn to pieces by vicious dogs, gassed and burnt in the crematoriums of Auschwitz, Majdanek, Bergen-Belsen, Buchenwald and dozens of other death camps — this was the fate of the Jewish people while a largely uncaring world turned a blind eye.

Nobel Laureate Elie Wiesel, himself a survivor, used one word to describe this period of bestiality: "Holocaust."

While many books, periodicals, docudramas, documentaries and movies have been produced about the Holocaust, not enough has been written or produced about the Righteous amongst the Nations. In the midst of the stygian darkness of Europe, these few, these Righteous, risked life and limb to save Jews. These noble and incredibly modest individuals defied the SS and their local followers who aided in the fiendish onslaught against the Jews.

To their everlasting glory they gave meaning to the words in Anne Franks's diary: "I still believe in the inherent goodness of mankind."

By their unselfish actions they have shown that not all of humankind sank into the pit of degradation and revulsion.

Victor Kugler, the central figure in this long overdue and much needed book, was just such a mild-mannered individual. Those who knew him in Holland and those who met him when he emigrated to Canada are unstinting in their praise of this humble man.

Kind, polite, respectful and unassuming are words that are often used to describe him. Certainly not a figure that one would call heroic and certainly not a Don Quixote tilting at windmills, but an ordinary citizen going about his everyday employment in the most ordinary of ways.

And yet, when the time came to act on behalf of his fellow humans he did not turn his back and walk away. Risking everything if his actions were discovered, and, at the very least, incarceration, he did not flinch from what he felt he must do. Without hope of reward of any kind he was the savior of the Franks until they were betrayed. How easy it would have been for Victor Kugler to inform on the whereabouts of the Franks and not only reap the gratitude of the Nazi thugs searching for Jews, but also to acquire the Franks' business once they were discovered.

But this was Victor Kugler and such actions were abhorrent to his very nature. It has been written in the Book of Proverbs "that righeousness exalteth a nation." How much more so does it exalt the individual.

Victor Kugler, you have been weighed in the balance and not found wanting. Your actions are an inspiration for all peoples.

This all-too-brief book should find a place of honor on every bookshelf and should be compulsory reading in every school.

— Sam Pasternak, National Commander,
Jewish War Veterans of Canada.

FOR ALL JEWISH WAR VETERANS WHO OFFERED THEIR LIVES IN THAT ANCIENT
AND UNFINISHED STRUGGLE FOR HUMAN FREEDOM AND DIGNITY

LES ANCIENS
COMBATTANTS
JUIFS DU
CANADA

JEWISH
WAR VETERANS
OF
CANADA

National Commander
Sam Pasternack

1995

With the outbreak of the second World War on September 1, 1939, the civilized
world was once again plunged into the cauldron of terror from which it would not
be able to extricate itself for six long years.

This was to be a war such as humankind had never experienced. All the evil
genius that the mind could devise, all the technological advances so painstakingly
developed over the past quarter century were to be directed towards ever greater
and more fearful destruction. Death came on land, in the air, on the sea and
under the sea. No one was safe. Military and civilian alike fell victim to the
onslaught of the "FOUR HORSEMEN OF THE APOCALYPSE".   Before this
conflict ended about 40 million people would be killed or murdered.

As evil as any war is, this one had an extra purpose and a special dimension, the
complete murder and destruction of European Jewry.   Aided and abetted by
certain segments of local populations in various countries, six million Jews were put
to death in the most horrifying manners imaginable.   Starved, beaten,.
experimented upon by deranged doctors, attacked and torn to pieces by vicious
dogs, gassed and burnt in the crematoriums of Auschwitz, Maijdanek, Bergen
Belsen, Buchenwald, and dozens of other death camps, this was the fate of the
Jewish people while a largely uncaring world turned a blind eye.

Nobel Laureate ELie Weisel, himself a survivor, used one word to describe this
period of bestiality, "Holocaust".

While many books, periodicals, docu-dramas, documentaries and movies had been
produced about the Holocaust, not enough has been written or produced about
the Righteous Amongst the Nations.   In the midst of the stygian darkness of
Europe, these few, these Righteous risked life and limb to save Jews.   These noble
and incredibly modest individuals defied the SS and their local followers who aided
in the fiendish onslaught against the Jews.

To their everlasting glory they gave meaning to the words in Anne Frank's diary "I
still believe in the inherent goodness of mankind."
By their unselfish actions they have shown that not all of humankind sank into the
pit of degradation and revulsion.

OFFICE: 1111 FINCH AVENUE WEST, SUITE 353, DOWNSVIEW, ONTARIO M3J 2E5 TELEPHONE: (416) 663-8387

Irving Naftolin : 1997

My father, Charles Wittenberg, was born in Lodz, Poland in 1914. He showed leadership qualities from his earliest years as illustrated by his forming and presiding over a sports club at the age of 14, whose membership numbered 2000 and whose vice president was a lawyer. Like many youth of his day, he was a member of the Communist Party but he was also one of the first to leave it as its injustices became known. He married my mother, Eve Pietrokowska, in 1937 and left Poland in 1939, urging other Jews to leave with him and arguing against the registration of Jews with the civic authorities. In France, he and my mother were members of the Maquis. He was hunted by the German occupiers who placed a price on his head for his work as head of false documentation, propaganda and anti-collaborationists for the province of Tarne. After the war he was widely hailed as a hero of the French underground and highly decorated. I was born in 1946 and in 1948 we came to Canada where my sister was born one month later. My father continued his campaigns against anti-Semitism and tyranny of all sorts. His quest for human justice and compassion for the needy was evident in his work on the town council of Mt. Forest, a small town where we lived for ten years. In the early 1960's, back in Toronto again, and in response to the resurgence of a neo-Nazi movement, he founded a party called N3: for Newton's third law - For every action there is an equal and opposite reaction. In the mid-1970's he was introduced to Victor and Lucy Kugler. They immediately became good friends. Recognizing Kugler's contribution to humanity as the protector of Anne Frank and also seeing his need for financial security, my father was instrumental in getting him the Heddy Munk prize. They remained friends, although Kugler soon began to show signs of the deterioration that was to take his life within a few years. For many years afterwards, until her death intervened, Lucy Kugler remained a close family friend. Throughout my father's life, both my parents continued to make appearances, to give talks and interviews and to demonstrate for a militant watchfulness against any encroachment of anti-Semitism into society.
  My father died in November 1993. My mother died in January 1995.

48 Warren Rd., Toronto   JEAN -VICTOR WITTENBERG.

Appendix 3

World War II: Comments by Irving Naftolin

From when the last World War ended in 1918, until 1933, Germany was a poor country, especially after the Depression of 1930.

How and where did Germany get the money to become big and strong, to build the biggest navy, army and air force? Thousands of soldiers, tanks, and airplanes, etc.?

From the German industrialists; from England and the US, who thought Germany would stop Russia from conquering Europe. That is what Hitler did.

The Western Allies forgot what Germany had done in the First World War.

In 1932, Hitler was elected chancellor of Germany. In 1933, he was chosen to be commander of the army. By 1939, Hitler had conquered five countries. The Western Allies appeased him. But when he invaded Poland in 1939 the Allies decided to fight back against the Germans. It was already too late to save Belgium, Holland and France, and almost too late to save England in 1940.

In April 1939, Italy joined Germany to form the Axis.

If the Allies had united before 1939, the war would have ended four years sooner.

After the war, VE Day, May 7, 1945, did the world know of the Nazis' heinous crimes? The truth surfaced. Six million Jews had been tortured and killed. Thirty million Christians had been killed. Millions more had been wounded. Many cities had been bombed. Many families in Europe were broken.

The world media, when reporting the Holocaust, suppressed, ignored or doubted that six million Jews were murdered and tortured, and their homes and businesses confiscated. There was little sympathy from Churchill; less from Roosevelt.

In the last fifty years the news media has behaved similarly. Regardless of the good Israel has done in terms of democracy, absorbing immigrants, technology, irrigation, defending itself from Arab murderers, helping poor countries, etc., Israel is the "pariah" country.

Forty years after the Nuremburg Laws of 1935, which relegated German Jews to fifth-class status, Elie Wiesel lectured at McGill University: "The opposite of love, education, law, is Indifference."

Victor Kugler, who helped to hide Anne Frank, was not indifferent.

Appendix 4

Letter from W. Gunther Plaut

One of the world's most prominent Reform Jewish theologians is German-born Rabbi W. Gunther Plaut of Toronto. He was one of the few German Jews fortunate enough to have emigrated from his land of birth soon after Hitler's accession to power. Toronto's Holy Blossom Temple, where Rabbi Plaut was the spiritual leader during the 1970s, was, as mentioned earlier, perhaps the first North American institution to interview Victor Kugler, which it did for its Brotherhood publication in 1958. Rabbi Plaut wrote to Mr. Naftolin in August 1996 in recognition of Mr. Naftolin's desire to complete Eda Shapiro's landmark project:

Dear Mr. Naftolin

I wish you success on your attempt to publish the Kugler memoir. Doing so will enlarge our knowledge of the Anne Frank saga and help us understand what it took to stand up to an implacable enemy.

Sincerely,

W.G. Plaut

from the study of

RABBI W. GUNTHER PLAUT, O.C., J.D.S., D.D., LL.D., H.LITT.D.
SENIOR SCHOLAR, HOLY BLOSSOM TEMPLE

21/8/96

Dear Mr. Naftolin,

I wish you success on your attempt to publish the Kugler memoir. Doing so will enlarge our knowledge of the Anne Frank saga, and help us understand what it took to stand up to an implacable enemy.

Sincerely,

W.G. Plaut

About the Compiling Editor

RICK KARDONNE is well known as both a journalist and a musical theater composer-lyricist-writer. Rick has written for the *Jewish Tribune* for over a decade, during which he interviewed such VIPs as Ariel Sharon, Binyamin Netanyahu, Shimon Peres, Mikhail Gorbachev, Lech Walesa, Wolf Blitzer, Gottfried Wagner (great-grandson of Richard) and, on a lighter note, Liza Minnelli.

Previously, Rick was music critic for the *Canadian Jewish News* for fifteen years. He has interviewed many other VIPs such as former US Secretary of State Al Haig and the late violinist Isaac Stern, for other publications such as the *Jewish Press* and Canada's *Financial Post*. Rick also compiled all research and musical material for *Elusive Summit*, the biography of the late Canadian classical pianist Sheila Henig.

He was cited by the Society of Canadian Magazine Writers for his article on the Joey and Toby Tannenbaum art donations to the Art Gallery of Ontario, which appeared in the spring 1996 issue of *Artfocus Magazine*.

As a composer-lyricist-writer, Rick has had six stage musicals produced in Canada, and in addition was a composer for Canada's second-longest-run-ever original musical, *Sweet Reason*. Rick also composed the original music soundtrack for the 1975 Toronto stage production of Sholem Aleichem's classic *Shver Tzu Zein a Yid*. He composed the original music soundtrack for Cayle Chemin's film *I Am Home*, which opened the Cape Town Film Festival of 1997, and besides having been screened several times on Vision-TV, WTN and CBC Maritimes, was screened at the 2002 International Jewish Genealogy Conference at Toronto's downtown Sheraton Centre.

Rick's songs have been both recorded and performed live by such Broadway actresses as Salome Bey and Louise Pitre as well as by the vocal coach for *Chicago*, Elaine Overholt. His choral anthem on the Entebbe rescue mission,

As in Days Gone By, after having been performed with a chorus and full orchestra at Toronto's Beth Emeth Bais Yehuda Synagogue, has been performed in Israel and England by the Beth Abraham Youth Chorale of Dayton, Ohio. Rick is married to the former Eda Golub, daughter of the late Cantor Gutman Golub of Bulawayo, Zimbabwe, and has two daughters, Tova and Mirra. He has been to Israel, where he has an extended in-law family, ten times.

Selected Bibliography

Abella, Irving, and Harold Troper. *None Is Too Many: Canada and the Jews of Europe 1933-1948*. Toronto: Lester and Orpen, 1982.

Amdur, Richard. *Anne Frank*. New York and Philadelphia: Chelsea House Publishers, 1993.

Brasz, Chaya, and Yosef Kaplan, eds. *Dutch Jews as Perceived by Themselves and by Others: Proceedings of the Eighth International Symposium on the History of the Jews in the Netherlands*. Leiden: Brill Publishers, 2001.

Dawidowicz, Lucy. *The War against the Jews, 1933-1945*. New York: Holt, Rinehart and Winston, 1975.

Frank, Anne. *Anne Frank: The Diary of a Young Girl*. Garden City, NY: Doubleday, 1952.

Gies, Miep. *Anne Frank Remembered: The Story of the Woman Who Helped to Hide the Frank Family*. New York: Simon and Schuster, 1982. (Large print: Boston: G.K. Hall, 1988.)

Keith, Janet. *A Friend among Enemies: The Incredible Story of Arie Van Mansum in the Holocaust*. Markham, Ontario: Fitzhenry and Whiteside, 1991.

Levin, Meyer. *The Obsession*. New York: Simon and Schuster, 1973.

Mihelich, Josephine R. *Andrew Peterson and the Scandia Story*. Minneapolis, MN: Copublished by the author and Ford Johnson Graphics, 1984.

Müller, Melissa. *Anne Frank: The Biography*. Translated by Rita and Robert Kimber. New York: Metropolitan Books/Henry Holt and Co., 1998.

Schnabel, Ernst. *Anne Frank: A Portrait in Courage*. New York: Harcourt Brace, 1958.